Let's Walk

AARON SEARCH

Two are better than one,
because they have a good reward
for their labor. For if they fall,
one will lift up his companion.

(Ecclesiastes 4:9 & 10.)

To my faithful wife and companion...
you have been a constant source of
strength and encouragement upon this
path that the Lord has laid before us.

Contents

Introduction

Backslide defined:

"to relapse into bad ways or error."

Dear backslider:

This is part of our daily battle as Christians. Because we're sinners, the prospect of being separated from God and finding ourselves in a backslidden condition is very real. At some point in our walk, most of us will give into some form of temptation in a time of weakness and be led astray. Therefore, we're told:

*Be sober, be vigilant; because your
adversary the devil walks about like a
roaring lion seeking whom he may devour.*
(1 Peter 5:8)

We have a supernatural enemy whose never-ending purpose is to disrupt the Lord's work in our lives. He's our greatest adversary and is not to be taken lightly. He's a deceiver, plotting always to infiltrate our minds with lies. He's supernatural and is thus capable of knowing our weakest areas, and he won't hesitate to exploit them. He is evil. He's a tempter. He's crafty at distracting us from the Spirit (blinding us) and appealing to our flesh. And then, to our dismay, we're lost to pride, fear, addiction, alcoholism, sexual immorality, lust of the eye and flesh, greed, complacency, etc. The list goes on and on as Satan sets out to snatch the Word out of the hearts of believers and choke our faith.

The good news is, no matter how big we've allowed our problems of sin to become, God is bigger:

*You are of God, little children, and have
overcome them, because He who is in you
is greater than he who is in the world.* (1
John 4:40)

"He who is in us" is the Holy Spirit. The Holy Spirit is God, and His power will not be usurped by the chief deceiver and his ploys, whose works have been ultimately destroyed:

He who sins is of the devil, for the devil has sinned from the beginning. For this purpose the Son of God was manifested, that He might destroy the works of the devil. (1 John 3:8)

This verse contrasts our two natures—that of the devil, which is sin, and the nature of Christ, which conquers sin. When we're practicing sin, we're corrupted and controlled by Satan. When we sin, we enter into rebellion and autonomy from God, and are found to be serving the father of lies.

Jesus came to free us from the works of Satan, and through Jesus we're reconciled to the Father of life. Brothers and sisters, we must break free of the devil's hold and return to the divine nature we were purposed for. We must do it *now*.

Therefore submit to God. Resist the devil and he will flee from you. (James 4:7)

I know you're thinking, *Easier said than done*— because I've been here. But it just seems so difficult because of the web of lies Satan has spun to corrupt our paradigm of faith. He's got us thinking that we need the sin we're doing to make us happy. Don't be deceived; that's a sham. Anything we take into ourselves outside of God is empty. Nothing other than the Holy Spirit will ever fill us up adequately. We can experience a true and lasting joy only when we're aligned with the purpose of our design.

Selfish grasping is exactly why Lucifer became Satan. God didn't create Satan; He created Lucifer, the "day star," and Lucifer became Satan when he fell. We're of Satan's nature in our fall. We weren't created to do the things we're practicing in our flesh now, and because this behavior is contrary to our design, we'll continue to reap death and destruction.

Let's make a decision now to realign ourselves with the Father through Christ. I promise the transition will not be as difficult as your mind sees it at the moment. It won't take long either. But it must begin with a step in the right direction. I, along with our Lord Jesus Christ, will be with you every step of the way.

Let's walk....

1

Prayer

Our first step is crucial. We must reestablish our communication link with God. This is the most important relationship we'll ever have, and we know that communication is necessary for any relationship to succeed.

Have you ever noticed that when we practice sin, our prayer life suffers? The first two things we stop doing is praying and reading our Bibles. We seem to think that when we sever these lines of communication, it's easier to pretend God isn't really there, and His instructions aren't really on us.

It's like playing hide-and-seek with toddlers. They don't really hide; they simply cover their eyes and think because they can't see you, you can't see them. That's childish.

There's no hiding from God, as we see in David's prayer:

> *Where can I go from Your Spirit? Or where*
> *can I flee from Your presence. If I ascend*
> *into heaven, You are there; if I make my*
> *bed in hell, behold, You are there.*
> (Psalm 139:7-8)

Though we can't hide from God, our sin will lead us into foolish reasoning. So, let me tell you with full confidence that God sees us, He loves us, and He wants nothing more than to reconcile our relationship with Him. He gave His only begotten Son to die on the cross for our reconciliation. Praise God for this opportunity!

Now is the time to act wisely. We mustn't give in to the voice of the tempter. Satan wants to try and convince us that we don't need to change anything right now, that we're fine as we are. He'll twist God's Word and have us believe that God will surely provide another opportunity for us later. Don't allow the father of lies to steal this moment.

> *Do not be deceived, God is not mocked; for*
> *whatever a man sows, that he will also*
> *reap.* (Galatians 6:7)

When we're in our sin, we're sowing to the flesh. God is a holy God and cannot partner with sin. What communion does light have with the darkness? None. So, in our sin, we're sowing corruption and death. How do we know that our sin won't leave us in dire straits tomorrow? We could find ourselves dead, in jail, fired from our job, or estranged from our spouse, our family, and friends. We can't be sure none of that will happen because we're not God, and we're unable to see the future. All we have control over is the moment we're currently in. So, let's seize it. Let's make the best of this moment before we find ourselves in a deeper darker place. Let's hit our knees and pray. And I don't mean just our physical knees; let's lay our hearts open before the Lord with all humility in preparation for Him to begin steadfast renovation. When we get to the place of repentance, I will confess my sin and you can confess your own. I'll pray with you:

Heavenly Father I come to you in the name of Jesus Christ my Lord and Savior. I thank You, Father, for Your love and patience. I thank You for this timely opportunity to reconcile my relationship to You and realign myself again with Your will. Thank

You, for everything You've done and everyone You've used to guide me here.

In the name of Jesus Christ I repent of my sins and ask You to forgive me. Father please forgive my selfishness and pride, and remember these transgressions no more. Father, I'm sorry for resisting You, for trying to get things and do things my way. I surrender these to You now along with any other selfish characteristics I've allowed to replace Your character. I surrender my pride, fleshly desires, fears, and addictions—that I may instead reap of Your Spirit and become available as a vessel of honor for You.

In the name of Jesus Christ, I ask You to pour Your Holy Spirit into me that I would be transformed into the person You're calling me to be. I thank You and praise Your name. Amen.

2

Repentance

If you sincerely prayed that prayer with me, we're now in a place where we can take action.

It begins with our mindset. For the process of renewing our minds, we'll take many things into account throughout the course of this book, but we must faithfully start with a mind of repentance. Repentance comes to our hearts when we realize the sin we've allowed to enter our lives. In our sin, we become separated from our Holy Father as we dishonor God and become inundated with guilt and shame. The onset of repentance stems from these feelings, then progresses to sincere remorse and regret, which lead to active repentance. That's where we are now—determining in our minds to turn from our sins (to literally make an about-face), and to pursue the will of our Father for our lives.

9

It starts in our minds, and then is manifested in our deeds. Repentance is total—a total change of our thoughts and of our way of living, the sooner the better. Listen to Jesus:

> *Remember how you received and heard; hold fast and repent. Therefore if you will not watch, I will come upon you as a thief, and you will not know what hour I will come upon you.* (Revelation 3:3)

Jesus here is warning the church at Sardis, but followers of Christ in any era do well to heed His warning. We can't forget the grace of God. He raised us from death in ourselves to life in Christ. We're set apart, purchased by the blood of our Lord to reconciliation with our Father. If we don't honor this grace, we'll be like the fool in Proverbs who returns to his folly like a dog returning to his own vomit.

We need God's grace and mercy. Without it, we leave ourselves open to the judgment of Christ. He'll come as a thief in the night, and we'll be caught off guard with the consequences of living nonrepentant.

The grace approach of our Lord is much preferable to the judicial approach. So, let's embrace an attitude of change and realign ourselves to God's design.

3

Joy and Patience

I've learned through the crowd of witnesses throughout the Bible and through my own experiences that we never want to take on any endeavor apart from God. The simple truth is that we can't manage anything good apart from God. Sure, we have our moments, but just the slightest opposition can and will disrupt us.

We were demonstrating self-control at work until our coworker threw us under the bus or had something negative to say about our work. We were patiently driving down the road until that guy cut us off and almost caused us to crash. We were happy in our relationship until our significant other had different ideas. We were joyful until cancer came, or we got laid off, or we became seriously hurt, or a family member died. This is the opposition I'm referring to—or as James terms it, *trials*. It's in the trial where we usually meet our limits, and if we don't look to the Lord, we unfortunately regress to our "old man" behavior.

> *But the fruit of the Spirit is love, joy, peace, patience, kindness, goodness, faithfulness, gentleness, and self-control. There are no laws against such as these.*
> (Galatians 5:22-23)

Apart from God, we cannot access the fruit of the Spirit. All these listed above are the characteristics of God and are available to us only through faith. When we don't respond to trials faithfully, we're reverting to our old nature in the flesh. It's here that we find ourselves doing what we don't want to do, as sin creeps in. We must keep faith to allow the full potential of God's power in our lives.

I know it's tough, because we're fleshly humans, and as humans we possess finite minds. That means we don't know it all, and although at times we'd like to think we do, we just don't. So, there will always be some mysteries for us until we return home.

Take Juan for example. He comes to the Mexican-American border on his bicycle, and he's got two large bags over his shoulders.

The border guard stops him and says, "What's in the bags?"

"Sand," answers Juan.

The guard says, "Well, we'll just see about that. Get off the bike."

The guard takes the bags and rips them apart. He empties them and finds nothing but sand. He detains Juan overnight while he has the sand analyzed, only to discover that it's nothing except sand. The guard releases Juan, puts the sand into new sandbags, heaves them up onto the man's shoulders, and lets him cross the border.

A week later, the same thing happens. The guard asks, "What have you got?"

"Sand," says Juan.

Again, the guard does his thorough examination and discovers that the bags contain nothing but sand. He gives the sand back to Juan, who crosses the border on his bicycle.

This sequence of events is repeated every week for three years. Finally, Juan stops showing up, so the guard goes looking for him and finds him in a cantina in Mexico. "Hey, buddy," says the guard, "I know you're smuggling something. It's driving me crazy—it's all I think about, and I can't sleep. Just between you and me, what are you smuggling?"

Juan takes a sip of his beer and says, "Bicycles."

Mystery revealed.

The guard got hung up on the sand. He was so blinded by it that he couldn't see the truth. That's what happens when our focus is consumed by our circumstances. We miss the solution. We get so distracted by our circumstances that we lose sight of the solution. The solution is always found in God—our faithful deliverer.

Life is full of curve balls. We'll face trials and struggles and problems that we have no answer for. As Christians we must exercise faith and wait upon the Lord. I promise He will have a better solution to our mysteries. However, most of us won't wait. We want immediate solutions to our adverse circumstances, and we'll accept almost anything in hope of finding relief: something tangible, something now—anything. Satan knows this, and it's about then that he shows up with a big bag of sand. He tells us the answer's in the sand; everything we need is there, and because it's right in front of us—we can see it—we settle for the sand.

But now, like the guard, we've come to understand: There's nothing in the sandbag but sand.

We end up with sandbags when we respond to life's trials with our flesh. We already know this, because the Bible tells us. We heard the preacher preach it, and the Holy Spirit is always trying to prompt us. We know—but our moment of weakness has developed over time into a hard-packed rut, and it's going to take more than the knowledge of truth to transform our paradigm. It's going to take the supernatural character of God to overcome this stronghold.

Let's walk with Brother James for a bit and learn how to increase our patience through faith and experience joy in the trial. James writes:

My brethren, count it all joy when you run into various trials, knowing that the testing of your faith produces patience. But let patience have its perfect work, that you may be perfect and complete, lacking nothing. If any of you lacks wisdom, let him ask of God, who gives to all liberally and without reproach, and it will be given him. But let him ask in faith, with no doubting, for he who doubts is like a wave of the sea driven and tossed by the wind. For let not

*that man suppose that he will receive
anything from the Lord; he is a double-
minded man, unstable in all his ways.*
(James 1:2-8)

James is speaking to the body of Christ. This word he gives to his "brethren" is exclusively for the family of God, and for good reason. Can you imagine telling a nonbeliever, "My brother, count it all joy when you fall into various trials"? He'd be like, "What? You want me to be happy about my undesirable circumstances?" No, for nonbelievers, a trial is only an obstacle. It's that thing standing in the way of their getting back to who they are. And who they are, in their eyes, is as good as it gets.

I can relate. Before accepting Christ, I would think in my pride, *I don't need anything or anybody.* I'm sure you can relate too. So we don't expect a nonbeliever to understand. And neither did James; hence that word "brethren." James is addressing the family of God, so this message is exclusively for us.

And He tells us, "My brethren, count it all joy when you fall into various trials." Now, as Christians—are we doing this?

Trials are inevitable, right? I can confidently presume that anyone reading this has gone through trials—or closer to the truth, is going through a trial now. Take a moment to reflect on a past or current period of trial. Maybe it was that time you got laid off, or when your kids were having some trouble. Or maybe it's relationship difficulties. Whatever it is, think back to the onset of that trial. Go back to the very beginning and try to recall the way you were feeling. Were you joyful at the prospect of what was coming your way, or had already befallen you? Did you start jumping for joy and high-fiving all your friends?

That's probably not the case for most of us. A lot of us don't really allow ourselves to feel joy until the blessing or deliverance arrives. Well, it doesn't have to be like that. There's no reason why any of us should have our joy stolen. That's Satan's ploy. Satan would have us believe that trials are synonymous with doom. *Oh no! What am I going to do now?*

When we manage our problems in the flesh, it's likely that we'll perceive them in a negative way, and sometimes even equate them with doom. This is the natural tendency of our thinking, and as a result we make things harder on ourselves. Remember Pharaoh? Although God was in his midst through the plagues and the preaching of Moses, he was still hard of heart. By the power of God, Pharaoh relented and allowed the Israelites to leave. But soon his fleshly mind got the better of him, and he wondered: "Who's going to do the work? Who's going to build? Who's going to cook? Who's going to clean? Where are my *slaves*?" So, he went back on his decision to let the Israelites go, and he took matters into his own hands. He didn't want these people leaving to worship and serve their God; he wanted them to worship and serve *him*. He assembled his army and chased after them, but he and his army were ultimately overthrown when God closed the Red Sea over them.

So, God's Word tells us,

> *Trust in the Lord with all of your heart, and lean not on your own understanding; in all your ways acknowledge Him, and He shall direct your paths.* (Proverbs 3:5-6)

This kind of trusting in God is impossible if we're self-serving. As A. W. Tozer portrays it in *The Radical Cross,* in every heart there's a throne; when self is on that throne, then Jesus is still on the cross; when self is on the cross, then Jesus is on the throne. If we want to experience true joy and have victory over our trials, we must yield to a power greater than ourselves. And yield totally; we're to trust in the Lord with all our heart—not some, but all.

We can't rationalize this, or else we'll talk ourselves right out of it. That's why the verse goes on to say, "Lean not on your own understanding." In our understanding reside evil and every selfish thing. We simply must have faith. Although a trial intruding into our life presents things we normally don't want to deal with, and goes against the intuition of our carnal nature, we must trust that God is going to do something remarkable in our lives through that trial—because He can. He will, and you can count on it, because unlike nonbelievers, we understand that the trial is not an obstacle but a platform. It's the place where God meets us, wherever that is, and He then exalts us from there.

James goes on to say something we're to *know*: "that the testing of your faith produces patience" (1:3).

In my trade—HVAC (heating ventilation and air conditioning)—I'm in the controls division. I install building management systems. Basically, the building owner and the engineer will first agree that their building would benefit from a building management system. The existing equipment, boilers, chillers, air handlers, exhaust fans, and VAV boxes are already there, for ten years maybe, but since replacing that equipment would cost hundreds of thousands of dollars, they call me out to put a system together that will better manage what they already have. We can put drives on fan motors and chillers that would create a soft start and stop, and it would save on equipment wear and the cost of replacement. We put sensors on everything and add schedules and alarms, so every stage of the mechanical process can be monitored and run as efficiently as possible. This saves on manpower, and also, more importantly, on energy.

Now before we turn the system over to the customer, we must first do a lot of testing to make sure we're controlling the equipment properly and efficiently. Each building is different in its specific design—a factory, retail store, restaurant, sanitation plant, etc.—so we must make sure we're meeting each customer's specific needs. Everything must be tested to show its value.

The money the customer invests into the upgraded system will come back to him. He gets it back in equipment repair and replacement costs, labor costs, and energy savings. They're always happy for the upgrade.

This is the same principle with our faith. Pay attention to this:

*Do you not know that your body is the
temple of the Holy Spirit who is in you,
whom you have from God? And that you
are not your own. For you were bought at a
price; therefore glorify God in your body
and in your spirit, which are God's.*
(1 Corinthians 6:19-20)

So, *we* are the building; God is the owner; and the uncomfortable trial that enters our life is construction of a new management system. The trial is the method God uses to fit us with an upgrade—a spiritual upgrade.

Spiritual upgrades are fruit of the Spirit. Look again at James 1:3: "knowing that the testing of your faith produces patience." Patience is a fruit of the Spirit; patience is an upgrade. James begins with patience because the blessing of patience helps us to maintain faith and to be able to wait on the Lord, as opposed to reacting in a fleshly manner.

You know what happens when we wait on the Lord? *Victory!* So, James goes on:

*But let patience have its perfect work, that
you may be perfect, and complete, lacking
nothing.* (1:4)

When I think of "perfect work," I'm immediately reminded of Jesus's ministry. He was about His Father's business day in and day out. He was faithful, obedient, and lacking nothing. Scripture tells us to first seek His kingdom and righteousness, and everything else will be added unto us. Jesus waited on the Father. God's perfect work is in His will, and is evident in the victories He provides. We saw it when David slew the giant. We saw it when Moses led Israel out of captivity. We saw it with Daniel in the lion's den. We see it throughout the Bible, and in history up to the present date. But even with such a great cloud of witnesses, we still don't always wait on the Lord. Instead of taking advantage of patience as our God-given upgrade, we impatiently take matters into our own hands.

You know what happens when we don't wait on the Lord? We're swimming! Imagine if Israel didn't wait on the Lord. The Red Sea is in front, Pharaoh's armies closing in from behind; there's nowhere to go. You start thinking: *There's no way I'm going back into slavery.* So instead of waiting for the miracle of the Lord in parting the Red Sea, you jump in and try to swim for it. You get out about a hundred feet, and fatigue sets in. The water starts feeling really cold, and the current is strong, and the waves rough and choppy. You're having trouble breathing, and then hypothermia sets in.

It's better to wait on the Lord. When we wait on the Lord, patience can have its perfect work.

James continues:

If any of you lacks wisdom, let him ask of God, who gives to all liberally and without reproach, and it will be given him. (1:5)

This sounds a lot like something Jesus tells us:

Ask, and it will be given to you; seek, and you will find; knock, and it will be opened to you. For everyone who asks receives, and he who seeks finds, and to him who knocks it will be opened. Or what man is there among you, who if his son asks for bread, will give him a stone, or if he asks for a fish, will he give him a serpent? If you then being evil, know how to give good gifts to your children, how much more will your Father who is in heaven give good things to those who ask him! (Matthew 7:7-11)

So *we*, as people with evil and selfishness in our hearts, still want nothing more than to give our children good things. Our Father in heaven, who is holy and has no evil in Him, wants to give His children good things: spiritual gifts and supernatural character! And therein lies the upgrade. We are the building, God is the owner. If we're lacking anything for our building to be complete, we need only to ask the Owner. He will give liberally and without reproach.

"But," says James,

let him ask in faith, with no doubting, for he who doubts is like a wave of the sea driven and tossed by the wind. (1:6)

The number one faith killer is doubt. Doubt hinders us from the joy and victory God intends for us. Remember when Jesus called Peter out onto the water? And Peter began walking on it—well, until doubt crept in. He began to notice the wind and waves and lost sight of Jesus. As Peter began to sink, Jesus took his hand and pulled him back up, saying, "O you of little faith, why did you doubt?" (Matthew 14:31). So, doubt will sink us.

Remember when Jesus was traveling from city to city, healing the lame, giving sight to the blind, and raising the dead? Everywhere He went, He performed miracle after miracle. And then He came to His own hometown and did few miracles there, because of the people's lack of belief. They had trouble seeing Him as Lord because they saw Him as someone else. They asked, "Isn't that Joseph and Mary's son, the carpenter?" If we don't see God as the miracle-maker, we won't see miracles. Nevertheless, lack of belief doesn't make God any less powerful; it just makes us less usable for the power of God.

Doubt also sounds like this: "God doesn't really care about me. With all the people in the world, why would he use me?" Or something like this: "I've sinned too much." Or, "My sin is too great." It's that little voice of insecurity Satan uses to tell us we're inadequate or unworthy of God's love. It's that insertion of doubt that robs us of joy and victory. It's all a lie. We are qualified in Christ.

Jesus, during His ministry, was perfect, complete, and lacking nothing, because of His abiding in the Father and the Father in Him. And He brings *us* into that abiding life as children of God:

> *Therefore, brethren we are debtors—not to the flesh, to live according to the flesh. For if you live according to the flesh you will die; but if by the Spirit you put to death the deeds of the body, you will live. For as many as are led by the Spirit of God, these are the sons of God. For you did not receive the Spirit of bondage again to fear, but you*

*received the Spirit of adoption by whom we
cry out, "Abba, Father." The Spirit Himself
bears witness with our spirit that we are
children of God, and if children, then also
heirs—heirs of God and also joint heirs
with Christ, if indeed we suffer with Him,
that we may also be glorified together.*
(Romans 8:12-17)

There it is. We too are sons and daughters of
God. We abide in Jesus, Jesus abides in the Father,
and the Father abides in us. Praise God!

*Therefore, if anyone is in Christ, he is a
new creation; old things have passed away,
behold all things have become new.*
(2 Corinthians 5:17)

Who we were is no more; we need to let that
person go, with all his doubt. That's where all the
tossing back and forth comes from. We can't reap in
the Spirit if we don't let go of the flesh. We *must* put
away the old man. We *must* put away the old
thinking. We're transformed by the renewing of our
minds. We are heirs to the kingdom. We belong to
the family of God. We're in to win!

But James says this about the one who doubts:

For let not that man suppose he will receive anything from the Lord. He is a double-minded man, unstable in all his ways.
(1:7-8)

Some of us think that prayer alone is enough—that if we just say the words, we're good. If those words aren't driven by faith, they're empty. The person who goes back and forth in their faith does not trust in the Lord and will by no means receive answered prayer from the Lord. When we come to the Lord in prayer, we must come in the confidence of faith. God honors the trust that we approach Him with.

The doubting and double-minded man James talks about is the person who's having trouble committing to new management. It's the person who will find no joy. It's not because they don't want to; I know, because I've been that person. I've been focused and at one with the Spirit, single-mindedly following Christ in faith, and then—*bam!* I'm confronted with a trial that ignites my pride and anger, and suddenly I'm double-minded. In only a moment, I've allowed a feeling to snap me out of my faith in the Spirit and into my flesh.

This is the product of having a double belief system. We have to decide who we're going to serve:

our way of doing things, or God's way. If we're wise, we choose God. However, if we allow ourselves to be derailed by our feelings, then we're reverting back to the person we were before we met Christ. This makes us unstable. We must not react to our flesh; we must be obedient to the Word of God. That is faith. Trusting our situation to God, in spite of the way we feel.

As Adrian Rogers says, faith believes in spite of circumstances, and obeys in spite of the consequences.

By faith we'll overcome our thoughts of fear and comply in the moment obediently. We can do this by selling out to do the right thing and then trusting the consequences to God.

For we walk by faith, not by sight.
(2 Corinthians 5:7)

So, we need to take our focus off the circumstance, and see past it to the victory that awaits us. It starts with our paradigm: knowing who God is and who we are in Him. Once we understand this, we can recognize our starting place.

Our starting place is victory. We can't lose because of who we are: children of God. We're in the family. We abide in Jesus, Jesus abides in the Father, the Father abides in us.

What does the Father have for us? Fruit of the Spirit—love, joy, peace, patience, kindness, goodness, faithfulness, gentleness, self-control. Supernatural power in the form of spiritual upgrades—all that we need to be perfect, complete, and lacking nothing.

We mustn't equate trials with doom. For the faithful Christian, the trial is a platform. This is where God does the work He must do in order to fit us with an upgrade. It doesn't always feel great in the midst of construction, but when we trust that He will see us through, we can hold onto our joy and endure our circumstances to God's glory.

Embrace it! Instead of praying for God to change your circumstances, ask Him to change *you* in the midst of your circumstances—because the situation we're asking God to change is usually something He's using to change *us.*

I read that scientists who were studying butterflies conducted an experiment involving butterflies completing the pupa stage (changing from caterpillar to butterfly inside the chrysalis), after which they normally must struggle and work to break free. When it was time for that to happen, the scientists instead cut away the chrysalis for them, setting them free. However, not a single one of them could fly. By not struggling to escape the chrysalis, the butterflies weren't afforded the opportunity to develop the muscles needed to operate their wings.

Struggling is part of the process. This is the same principle in our struggle as Christians. Sometimes we need to go through things so we can develop our spiritual muscles. If we choose to duck and dodge the circumstances that come with a struggle instead of pressing on in faith, our faith won't get the opportunity to develop in the test—and we will never fly.

4

Works

Now, let's take a step in faith and do a little work. We know our faith is genuine when we honor God in our work. Let's honor God now by taking steps to rid our lives of the sin and temptations that hinder our walk. Prayer should always precede any work we attempt. We would be remiss to not include our faithful Guide when taking anything on. Let's pray:

Heavenly Father, I thank You for Your counsel through Your Spirit and Word. I thank You for this opportunity to change, so I come to You in my time of need. You see the sin in my life and are already aware of my need. I ask You now to bless me with the strength, courage, and integrity I need to remove the temptations and sins from my life. I surrender my will, and I ask in Jesus's name that Your will be done in this matter. Amen.

Set this book down this very moment and extinguish the paraphernalia of your sin. If it's drugs, alcohol, prescription pills, etc.—flush them now. If it's magazines, DVDs, websites, etc.—shred or destroy or delete them now. If it's a sinful relationship, delete the contact and terminate the relationship now. Whatever tempts you to sin, you must cast it out now. Remove it from the physical, mental, and spiritual premises now. Do not think; do not fear; do not give way to your understanding or feelings. Simply act obediently in faith and trust the consequences to God.

Sin is serious. It goes directly against the manifestation of Christ and what He came to do. Sin is rebellion against God.

> *For you, brethren, have been called to liberty; only do not use liberty as an opportunity for the flesh, but through love serve one another.* (Galatians 5:13)

Even though we've secured our salvation, we aren't at liberty to sin. In sin we oppress the power of the Holy Spirit and separate ourselves from God. While in sin, we're creating opportunities in the mind for our flesh, and we're unavailable to serve one another through love because all we love is ourselves. This is contrary to our Creator's design for us, so we ultimately find ourselves in the place we are now—dissatisfied and unhappy as we're separated from God.

5

Self-Control

Now that we've removed the paraphernalia of our sin, we can move forward. This will be an impossible transition if we try to do it on our own. We've come this far by the grace of God, and we'll continue to progress in victory only by His grace.

So, it's a good day to be Christian, and I'll tell you why: because of *self-control.*

Self-control is fruit of the Spirit, and therefore it's accessible only for the person in Christ. Praise God! What a valuable commodity for the believer to possess! In fact, for a lot of us, it was our glaring lack of self-control that brought us to the realization of our need for Christ. Before, we'd been thinking we were all-powerful and in control, because the number one misconception we have is believing that controlling myself to restrain my sinful desires is something *I* do.

The Greek philosopher Plato believed that controlling one's appetites and passions was possible through instructed reason and the power of the will. Plato isn't alone in his thinking. I believe we've all thought that way at some point in our lives. We liked to believe we were self-sufficient—that *we got it.*

The New Testament, however, teaches us that true self-control is the fruit of the Spirit in the life of the believer. It's a control from within, a control of self, but it's by and through the Holy Spirit's enabling. Praise God for His wisdom! He knows what we lack, so He makes it available to us. That's an upgrade. And I liken all fruit of the Spirit as such, because we came into this world in base form.

Take a car lot, for example. There are new cars everywhere, but they aren't all the same. Some have all the bells and whistles, others have fewer upgrades, and then there's the base model. We are the base model—just enough to get around in this world by the world's standard, but it's not until we come into God's kingdom that we can be fitted with a spiritual upgrade. To us as Christians, self-control has now become available. So now we have to ask, Why does God want to fit us with this upgrade?

Paul Harvey told a story on how Eskimos sometimes killed wolves. A knife with a razor-sharp edge was soaked in blood, then frozen. After repeating that process numerous times, the blade would be completely concealed in frozen blood. It was then stuck blade up into the frozen ground, waiting for a wolf to catch its scent. The attracted wolf, unable to quench its desire for blood, would ultimately bleed to death from wounds inflicted by licking the blade.

That's a perfect example of being consumed by one's own lusts. I'm sure some of us have been the wolf but were fortunate to have been rescued by God's saving grace. And I suspect that we all have known someone who has been completely consumed to death.

Upon accepting Christ, we become new creations, and we quickly learn through separating ourselves from old habits just how vital self-control is to maintaining spiritual growth. Our old self—or as Paul says, "the old man"—dies with Christ and is buried, and the new man is resurrected with Christ. We're made new, and old things have passed away.

God immediately gives us the Holy Spirit, and we begin our transformation the very moment we ask Christ to be our Savior. This is God's free gift; our only participation is to repent, confess our sin, acknowledge that Jesus died on the cross for our sin, and then take Him to be our Savior, in all sincerity. We're now heirs of the kingdom and are indwelt by the Holy Spirit. We're made new!

Going forward, we must increase our level of participation. We must utilize our supernatural upgrades (fruit of the Spirit) that God has made available to us if we're to mature to God's glory. If not, we'll resort back to the familiarity of our flesh, and we'll lose the struggle in breaking away from the old man.

Christians who lack self-control are stunting their own growth. Sure, we exercise great self-control when it comes to our appearances. On the outside we look like we have it all together, but on the inside, we lack self-control in moral areas such as sexual infidelity and dishonesty in our personal and business relationships. Without self-control, it's impossible to walk with God in any great degree, or to grow into a mature Christian. There can be no great faith, great love, or great spiritual fire for God without self-control. The greatness we long to know comes only from God's power.

Without the fruit of self-control, we can't manage ourselves appropriately, including our finances, our time, our habits, our emotions, or even our ability to overcome temptation. How will the character of God be manifest in us if we can't control ourselves in word and deed? It takes the grace of God to overcome our wayward tongue and temper with a kind word and a generous deed.

Without self-control, how would we be able to find the time we need to grow in our personal relationship with Christ, dedicating ourselves to Him in His Word and prayer? There's no other relationship above this one. Are we treating our relationship with Him as priority, or are we giving way to idolatry? We shouldn't put anything before God.

A few years ago, my wife and I picked up a friend on our way to church. Along the way we discussed biblical solutions to some of life's everyday problems. My friend started shaking his head and told me that I didn't understand. I asked him to help me understand, and he said, "You have a simple answer for everything. But everything isn't that simple. Sometimes there are gray areas."

I said understood, and I agreed that there are indeed gray areas—and added that there are biblical solutions to that too. I asked him if he was reading his Bible. He said, "Not as much as I should." I suggested that he read it more if he wanted clarity, and that the Bible is unmistakably clear—it's black and white, while it's *us* who are the gray area. This truth hit home with him, and he pledged to spend more time in God's Word.

Recently I spoke to him again. The first ten minutes of our conversation was his sharing a barrage of injustices he couldn't understand. I asked him if was going to church. His said there wasn't one near him. I asked if he'd been praying about this. He replied, "Probably not as much as I should." I asked if he was reading his Bible. He said he'd just looked at it the other day and thought about reading it some.

Fellowship, prayer, God's Word—in any one of these we can find deliverance to the glory of God, but sometimes we lack the discipline and self-control to prioritize these in our lives. Praise God for His wisdom, but unless we apply it, it's only of informational value. He provides a way for us to rise above our flesh.

Billy Graham, in his message on "The Christian's Inner Struggle between Two Natures," tells about a fisherman who came to town every Saturday afternoon. He always brought his two dogs with him, one white and the other black. He'd taught them to fight each other on command. Every Saturday afternoon in the town square, people would gather, and the two dogs would fight while the fisherman took bets. Sometimes the black dog would win, and sometimes the white dog, but the fisherman always won. His friend asked him how he did it. The fisherman replied, "I starve one and feed the other. The one I feed always wins, because he's stronger."

That story speaks to the inner warfare that comes into the life of a person who's born again. We have two natures within us, both fighting for control. Which one will dominate us? It all depends on which one we feed.

Since we are living in the Spirit, let us follow in the Spirit's leading in every part of our lives. (Galatians 5:25)

There's a great peace when we're in tune with God's Spirit. We've all experienced it—that goodness, that contentment, when we've surrendered the moment, and we're walking step for step in the path our Creator has laid before us.

It's only when we step out of alignment with God's will that we encounter a break in contentment. It's never because we come across a tough patch in God's path; His way isn't tricky, and it doesn't veer to the left or right. No, the steps He has for us are clearly laid out directly in front of us.

It's only when I experience a lapse of self-control that I find myself deviating from the path. I'll be content, doing just fine in my walk, in tune with the Holy Spirit and praising God, when out of nowhere I'll let some fear consume my thoughts. For example, I once recalled how a project manager at work made a general comment along the lines of how the quality of workmanship these days isn't the same as it used to be. This wasn't directed toward me, but inwardly I asked, *Could he be talking about me? Is he talking about one of my projects?* With such thinking, if I'm not careful, I allow a feeling of insecurity to knock me off the path. I'm no longer content; the feeling of goodness is gone. I go from walking along a clear and stable path to hiking in the bushes, getting my legs scratched up, and stepping in gopher holes. My peace is snatched away because I failed to utilize the Spirit's enabling power of self-control when I came across an undesirable feeling.

Can I blame my emotions for distracting my walk? Sure, but that won't resolve anything, and leads only to other undesirable feelings. Should I try and desensitize myself and become disconnected from my emotions so they can't hinder me further? Of course not. Our emotions are a big part of our makeup. The Bible tells us we're made in God's image, and God's emotions are evident in His anger toward sin and His great love for us.

So, we see how important it is that we learn to manage our emotions rather than allowing them to manage us. Anger can be a huge stumbling block for me if I don't practice self-control. So, when I feel anger welling up inside me, it's important that I stop whatever I'm doing in that moment and identify that I'm angry, then examine my heart to determine *why* I'm angry, and then proceed in a biblical manner. It starts with recognition, then I look to Jesus to help me behave obediently in faith in spite of the way I'm feeling.

Paul tells us in 2 Corinthians that we're to bring every thought into captivity to the obedience of Christ. This doesn't happen with a snap of the fingers. It takes training. Let's walk with Brother Paul for a bit and learn some biblical training. Paul writes,

Do you not know that those who run in a race all run, but one receives the prize? Run in such a way that you may obtain it. And everyone who competes for the prize is temperate in all things. Now they do it to obtain a perishable crown, but we for an imperishable crown. Therefore I run thus; not with an uncertainty thus I fight; not as

one who beats the air. But I discipline my
body and bring it into subjection, lest when
I have preached to others, I myself should
be disqualified. (1 Corinthians 9:24-27)

That passage begins with a picture from the world of athletics. The term "athlete" is from an ancient Greek word that means one who competes for a prize. Before the nineteenth century there weren't any distinctions between amateur or professional; all who competed were simply athletes.

In Paul's time, there weren't team competitions like we have today. All the sports games were individual contests, such as foot races, long jumping, wrestling, boxing, and discus and javelin throwing. Awards were given in each event for the one athlete who conquered his opponents. There were no runner-up trophies and no ribbons just for participating. There was only one prize for the one athlete who won the event.

Paul tells us we should run in such a way that we're the one who obtains the prize. Second or third place isn't good enough. So, we shouldn't be content just to finish; we want to finish as the winner. Paul isn't suggesting that winning is everything; he's simply saying we must run with the attitude of the victor. We want to run with the faith and determination that victory requires.

Paul adds that "everyone who competes for the prize is temperate in all things"; the athlete does this "to obtain a perishable crown," while we, as Christians practicing self-control, are seeking "an imperishable crown" (9:25). Temperance is synonymous with self-control. Athletes condition their bodies by controlling their diet and managing their training regimen and mental paradigms. They do this with focused determination and sacrifice to meet a goal. That goal is the prize, the driving force of their convictions. However, the athlete's prize—the crown—is perishable. But the crown Christians strive for is not of this world. We run with and for Christ to reign with Christ.

"Therefore," Paul says, "I run thus; not with uncertainty. Thus, I fight; not as one who beats the air" (9:26). Paul runs with conviction, buffeting his body as a whole to withstand anything rising up against the gospel. His attitude carries over into the way he fights. Paul's athletic imagery here has changed from running to boxing, but the determination and sacrifice in how he fights is still there. The Christian trains with a purpose—with steady focus, and with no wasted movements. We fight as one who does not beat the air. We all know what a natural man looks like when fighting—just a bunch of out-of-control testosterone aimlessly beating the air in front of him. A boxer, however, is trained; his movements are concise and not wasted. Likewise, the trained Christian uses his reach to keep sin back, and keeps his guard up against temptation. He ducks away from incoming deceptions and counters any feelings that stem from his flesh in opposition to God's will.

Paul then concludes, "I discipline my body and bring it into subjection, lest when I have preached to others, I myself should be disqualified" (9:27). Here Paul states how he has aligned himself to best deliver the good news. And isn't that what it comes down to for Christians? It's our inherent duty to point others to Christ. We prepare ourselves through spiritual upgrades—such as self-control—to discipline our attitude for a life spent sharing the gospel. The conduct of a Christian is what gives or takes power from our testimony. Do our actions collaborate with our beliefs, and thus qualify our proclamation of the gospel? When I bear witness, do others see and hear only me, or do they see and hear the power of God in me? There's a big difference, because it's the power of God that draws the lost to Christ.

This is why we must discipline ourselves and take on the fruit of the Spirit that is self-control. The profound path of faith isn't easy; it demands that we persevere and endure, pushing past our weariness as we approach the finish line.

6

Peace

We've adjusted our paradigm and have begun looking to God. In our repentance we've reestablished our communication link with our Creator, and we now have access to God Almighty's power in our lives. By the fruit of the Spirit we can overcome Satan's influence, the world, and ourselves. Now, how do we maintain all this? We maintain it by living according to the way we were designed. The sooner we transition our daily walk to align with God's will, the sooner we'll experience the peace that surpasses all understanding.

We see that peace is a fruit of the Spirit. It comes from God, so it's a supernatural upgrade that will indeed surpass our understanding. That peace is on us when we're experiencing the satisfaction of our needs being met. Unless we keep the faith, we lose peace when we're met with affliction, when the sustenance to maintain life and shelter for our well-being is in jeopardy. We must therefore hold onto valuable truths and not waver. We must believe that all of God's promises are true and that He has a plan for every one of us.

Well, again, it's a good day to be a Christian. We have exclusive access to the Prince of peace Himself. His peace for us is not just temporary or conditional, like what the world has to offer. No, for the person born of God, there is true peace, lasting peace, a peace that surpasses all understanding. Our Lord says,

> *My peace I give to you; not as the world do I give to you. Let not your heart be troubled, neither let it be afraid.* (John 14:27)

We have peace in His Word. What the Lord teaches us is not opinion; it's foundational truth that's set in conviction. We change our opinions at will, but our convictions stick with us. So when things of this world present trouble, we have no need to be either troubled or afraid. We need only look to the promises of His Word to strengthen our resolve.

Years ago a farmer who owned land along the Atlantic coast was seeking hired hands, but he found that potential laborers dreaded the awful Atlantic storms that wreaked havoc on farm buildings and crops.

He advertised for help but received few inquiries. However, one man—small and middle-aged—came and sought the job.

"Are you a good farmer?" the farmer asked.

"Well," answered the little man, "I can sleep when the wind blows."

The farmer was puzzled by this answer, but being desperate for help, he hired the man.

The little man worked well around the farm, staying busy from dawn to dusk, and the farmer felt satisfied. Then late one night, a howling wind awakened the farmer. Jumping out of bed, he grabbed a lantern and rushed to the hired hand's sleeping quarters. He shook the little man and yelled, "Get up! A storm's moving in! Tie things down before they blow away!"

The little man only rolled over in his bed. "No sir," he said firmly, "I told you, I can sleep when the wind blows."

Enraged by this response, the farmer hurried outside to do the necessary work himself. But to his amazement, he discovered that all the haystacks had been covered in tarpaulins, and the cows in the barn were safe behind barred doors, as were the chickens were in their coops. The shutters on the house windows were tightly secured. Everything was tied down. Nothing could blow away. The farmer then understood what his hired hand meant. He returned to his bed to also sleep while the wind blew.

His hired hand was able to sleep because he'd secured the farm against the storm. We, as believers in Christ, secure ourselves against the storms of life by grounding ourselves in the Word of God.

The New Testament speaks of two kinds of both objective peace and subjective peace. Objective peace has to do with our relationship with God.

In Romans 5:10, Paul tells us that we were enemies of God. Everything we did opposed His principles. This opposition occurred at the very beginning. Remember Adam and Eve? God gave them a beautiful garden to live in, called Eden. In it were all the fruits and vegetables they could enjoy. They had dominion over all this and all the animals. It was paradise. They lived in perfect peace, until they disobeyed one rule. God had given them permission to enjoy the food from every plant and tree except for one, the tree of the knowledge of good and evil. God also clearly explained to them that if they ate from this tree they would die.

This created the first opportunity for man to oppose God. Satan recognized this opportunity and came to Eve in the form of a serpent. He then deceived Eve. Both Eve and Adam ate of the forbidden fruit, and sin was born. Ever since then, human beings are separated from God—He's over there in His holiness, and we're over here in our sin. But our gracious God provided a way to bridge that gap. Through Jesus's work on the cross, we're made righteous in the sight of God, and now, as believers, we're again at peace with God. There's no peace apart from God. Praise God!

Subjective peace is a goodness of life that isn't touched by what happens on the outside. That means we can be in the midst of great trials and still have peace. Without peace we can't experience the joy James told us about.

Let's walk a bit with Luke and see how the peace that Jesus offers delivers a woman who couldn't find peace anywhere else.

Now a woman, having a flow of blood for twelve years, who spent all of her livelihood on physicians and could not be healed by any, came from behind and

*touched the border of Jesus' garment. And
immediately her flow of blood stopped.*

And Jesus said, "Who touched Me?"

*When all denied it, Peter and those with
Him said, "Master, the multitudes throng
and touch You, and You say, 'Who touched
Me?'"*

*But Jesus said, "Somebody touched Me, for
I perceived power going out from Me." Now
when the woman saw that she was not
hidden, she came trembling; and falling
down before Him, she declared to Him in
the presence of all the people the reason
she had touched Him and how she was
healed immediately.*

*And He said to her, "Daughter, be of good
cheer, your faith has made you well, go in
peace."* (Luke 8:43-48)

Here we have a woman who has been suffering
an affliction for over a decade, and she's therefore
unable to find peace. She has spent everything she
had on doctors to free her from this bondage, and
they could not. Doctors possess training and
medicines to heal, but in this particular case they
could not. This is sometimes true today. Doctors
simply don't have all the answers to people's mental

and physical needs. Sometimes all a doctor can do is to prescribe you something that might lessen the effect of your symptoms and give you temporary relief, though probably not without side effects.

Meanwhile, self-medicating is a poor choice for those who can't afford professional help or simply don't have medical insurance. It happens; there are many temporary solutions in the world of self-medication. However, solutions like that have a dark side of their own, and one could end up worse than they were at the beginning.

I'm sure this woman in her twelve years of suffering ventured down many paths in search for relief. This is where desperation leads us. To her great fortune, the Messiah crossed her path. Like many of us, she'd heard that Jesus was accessible and that He possessed the power to heal. This had been proclaimed from town to town and city to city. It was known. And she believed that if she could just touch the edge of His garment, she could be delivered. In her desperation she turned to Jesus to stop the bleeding. This woman "came from behind and touched the border of Jesus' garment" (8:44).

I get that. I grew up with a severe case of ADHD that ultimately stunted my emotional and social growth. It led to loneliness, which led to poor friendship choices. That led to drugs and alcohol, which led to criminal activity, which led to a life in prison. Finally, five years into a twenty-year sentence, I took a good look at myself and saw that I was a deplorable man. I didn't want to be that man anymore, so I put effort into making a change. I tried NA and AA. I read self-help books, psychology books, and books on the power of this and that and the other thing. I exhausted the worldly resources at my disposal and reaped little benefit. I figured I was just wired wrong, and I was destined to spend my life in prison. I was broken.

Like the woman, I heard about Jesus. He wasn't my first choice, but eventually I had nowhere else to turn. He was my last hope, so I turned to Him in desperation. I didn't approach Him with the same faith the woman did. On the contrary, I barely opened my heart a crack. But that was all Jesus needed. He stepped right on in and stopped the bleeding, just as He did for her.

> *And immediately her flow of blood stopped. And Jesus said, "Who touched Me?"...Peter and those with Him said, "Master, the multitudes throng and press You, and You say, 'Who touched Me?'"(8:44-45)*

Jesus knew. In Matthew's account of this event, we read that Jesus "turned around," and "He saw her" (Matthew 10:22). Jesus is the One who says, "I am the good shepherd, and I know My sheep" (John 10:14). The moment you place your faith in Jesus—He knows!

By asking, "Who touched Me?" in Luke 8, He was calling out this woman to testify to her healing from Him: "Somebody touched Me, for I perceived power going out from Me" (Luke 8:46).

See how the woman touched Him and received immediate healing. She believed that He is who He says He is, and that He possesses the power to heal. Jesus did not withhold this power from her. Why would He? People of faith—those of us believing that Jesus is who He says He is, and that He *can*—are exactly the people who He has power for.

> *Now when the woman saw that she was*
> *not hidden, she came trembling; and falling*
> *down before Him, she declared to Him in*
> *the presence of all the people the reason*
> *she had touched Him and how she was*
> *healed immediately.* (8:47)

This is the result Jesus desired when He asked, "Who touched Me?" He desires this result in every one of us. Whether it's addiction, depression, anger, fear and insecurities, a bad relationship, sickness and disease—whatever it is, surrender it to Jesus.

Hold nothing back. We need Jesus to stop the bleeding, and upon deliverance we're to declare in the presence of all the people how we reached out to Jesus and were healed. We're to testify to the power of Christ in our lives. This is how we share the kingdom. This is how we save lives to the glory of God according to His will.

> *And He said to her, "Daughter, be of good cheer, your faith has made you well, go in peace."* (8:48)

Jesus's solution to troubling life circumstances is for us to bring our concerns to Him in prayer and to trust in Him:

> *Be anxious for nothing, but in everything by prayer and supplication, with thanksgiving, let your requests be made known to God; and the peace of God, which surpasses all understanding, will guard your hearts and mind through Christ Jesus.* (Philippians 4:6-7)

We live in a fallen world filled with turmoil and injustice, in which Satan is prowling around seeking whom he may devour. The world and its sicknesses can be one great stumbling block after another if we don't stay grounded in the Word and maintain our faith. God is the Rock, and if we stand in Him, we will not be moved:

> *Cast your burden on the Lord, and He shall sustain you; He shall never permit the righteous to be moved.* (Psalm 55:22)

Let me tell you a story told by Max Lucado about Lloyd Douglas. When Lloyd was in college, he lived in a boarding house. On the first floor resided a retired music teacher who was crippled and unable to leave his apartment. He and Lloyd had a morning ritual; Lloyd would come down the stairs, open the man's door, and ask, "Well, what's the good news?" The old man would pick up his tuning fork, tap it on the side of his wheelchair, and say, "That's middle C; it was middle C yesterday, it will be middle C tomorrow, and it will be middle C a thousand years from now. The tenor upstairs sings flat, the piano across the hall is out of tune, but my friend, that is middle C." The old man had discovered a constant reality on which he could depend, an unchanging truth to which he could cling.

Jesus is the middle C of the soul. In a world of competing truths, His pitch defines reality and sets every note in its proper place. Jesus Christ is the same yesterday, today, and forevermore. Because

He's the middle C, you can hear the music in heaven even when you're going through hell on earth. It's in Jesus that we can find peace in spite of our poor experiences here on earth.

Peace is not our greatest need; it's a blessing. It's the manifestation of God's character in us. The Blesser is our greatest need! Praise God for recognizing our greatest need where we could not. As Charles Sell has expressed it, if our greatest need was to have pleasure, God would have sent us an entertainer; if our greatest need was for us to have technology, He would have sent us a scientist; if our greatest need was to have money, he would have sent us an economist. However, our greatest need was for forgiveness—so He sent us a Savior.

Some of us will overlook the Blesser because we only want the blessing. We mustn't put the cart before the horse. Jesus made it possible with His work on the cross to reconcile us with the Blesser. Praise the Lord! It's the communion of this relationship that leads to peace.

7

Goodness

G od is evident in our lives when we experience
joy and peace in the midst of our trials, and
when we faithfully exercise patience and self-
control in spite of our circumstances. We no longer
pursue carnal satisfaction, because we're Spirit-
minded and seek to serve our Creator. We're
available and usable for God in this condition of
surrender and faith, and as a result we start
extending the goodness of God that has been
extended to us. This is the unstoppable consequence
of "less me and more God."

When you think about it, less me and more God
is a good trade-off, considering that God is good and
we're not. As we walk in this world, we must be
careful not to resort back to the world's standards.

We mustn't forget that we're set apart, and that we'll need to call upon God's grace through His spiritual upgrades.

The Bible tells us that we need to be on the narrow road. On this road, as it runs contrary to the direction of the world, we will be met with opposition:

> *Enter by the narrow gate; for wide is the gate and broad is the way that leads to destruction, and there are many who go in by it. Because narrow is the gate and difficult is the way which leads to life, and there are few who find it.*
> (Matthew 7:13-14)

Jesus teaches this directly. He says we're to go against the grain and to not be conformed to this world. The wide gate and broad road are easier to follow, and we'll fall in line there with the many, unless the grace of God redirects us.

We're therefore wise to continually seek God's goodness in us. We can do this through self-examination. Psalm 119:59 tells us to consider our ways—a spiritual diagnostic examination, if you will—so we can stay in line with His testimonies. This means we should be aware of our situational encounters in the moment and the recent past and weigh the conduct of our hearts to see if they're in line with the Holy Spirit. If we're walking in faith, there will undoubtedly be works to support God's presence. I guarantee it.

Another reason we must examine ourselves spiritually is that something terrible could be going on inside us that's undetectable without an examination. For example, I heard about a middle-aged man was running in a marathon. He was one of the front-runners as the finish line neared—which wasn't surprising, since he was in great shape from competing in marathons throughout his life. In this race, he finished strong, among the top ten. But four minutes later, he collapsed and died. This came as a shock to all who knew him, because he was such a physical specimen who took great care of himself. The autopsy revealed a condition in his heart that was treatable, and had he been treated for it, he would probably still be alive and running today. But because he appeared healthy, he saw no reason to take the physical diagnostic examination that would have saved his life.

This can be the case with our spiritual health also. We may appear to be fine on the outside while on the inside we're slowly slipping away, so slowly and subtly that we might not notice without a thorough examination.

It's similar (as someone once told me) to how a cow gets lost. The cow grazes on a little patch of grass here, then moves over there to another patch. Then she finds a patch by the fence. There's an opening in the broken fence, and the cow sees a patch of grass beyond it—so off she goes. Likewise, we take in a little sin here and there, and before you know it, we're lost.

The goodness of God is clearly seen throughout the Bible in the grace and generosity and abundant love He shows us. He is faithful to meet our needs, which is fortunate for us because our needs are many, and fully meeting them is impossible apart from God.

And trying to fully do good without first being good is impossible. History shows that Hitler enjoyed taking pictures with his dog. From the pictures you can tell that he really loved his dog and cared for it. To be able to faithfully care for an animal is a good act, yet we know that Hitler was far from good. This is the case for all people; we're certainly capable of managing good things here and there—even the worst of us. But because of our nature, we aren't consistently good in many areas of our lives.

For us, badness comes naturally:

Because the carnal mind is enmity against God; for it is not subject to the law of God, nor indeed can be. (Romans 8:7)

But goodness starts with God; genuine goodness is a virtue (a spiritual upgrade) that pours into us from our relationship with God:

Do you despise the riches of His goodness, forbearance, and longsuffering, not knowing that the goodness of God leads you to repentance? (Romans 2:4)

This is where we begin to consciously take God's goodness into our lives—as at the beginning of the book when we repented, or for the person who receives Christ as his Savior. It's when God begins to separate us from the badness of our nature. We're exposed to His goodness as we're made righteous by Christ. In His goodness, He does not will the death of sinners; instead He is patient with us. Praise God! How patient are we with others? Good thing I'm not God; no one would stand a chance in my kingdom.

Death is for the wages of sin, but God is good to us in allowing us time for our rebellion to pass and for us to recognize our need for salvation. When we establish our need for a relationship with God, we can reap the extended benefits of His goodness:

*Do not be conformed to this world, but be
transformed by the renewing of your mind,
so that you may prove what is that good
and acceptable and perfect will of God.*
(Romans 12:2)

We now begin the transformation process from our imperfect will to God's perfect will. We stop walking with the world and start walking with the Lord. We stop moving by the inclination of what our minds perceive through our flesh (sight), and we begin moving forward by the inclination of what the Spirit and God's Word would have us believe (faith). Through our faith, God can manifest the extent of His goodness in our lives, because faith gives rise to a supernatural quality in our soul that brings about good action.

Now let's walk with Brother James again and learn how God in His goodness manifests His works through our faith:

*What does it profit, my brethren, if
someone says he has faith but does not
have works? Can faith save him? If a
brother or sister is naked and destitute of
daily food, and one of you says to them,
"Depart in peace, be warmed and filled,"
but you do not give them the things that
are needed for the body, what does it profit?*

Thus also faith by itself, if it does not have works, is dead.

But someone will say, "You have faith and I have works." Show me your faith without your works, and I will show you my faith by my works. You believe that there is one God. You do well. Even the demons believe—and tremble!(James 2:14-19)

I love Brother James. He doesn't mince words. His revelations in the Holy Spirit are blunt, and I believe that's a good thing. There's nothing soft or light about the fact that faith without works isn't really faith at all. What does faith without works profit? Nothing! Can faith save him? *No!* A faith without the unstoppable reaction of works is useless.

Whoever falsely boasts of giving is like clouds and wind without rain.
(Proverbs 25:14)

Without God we have nothing good to give. A faith with corresponding works is full where a faith without works is empty. Empty faith is not genuine faith, so it's correct to presume that the person with empty faith never really took God into their lives. A relationship with Jesus Christ will bear fruit.

Let's take a closer look at what James says here:

> *If a brother or sister is naked and destitute*
> *of daily food, and one of you says to them,*
> *"Depart in peace, be warmed and filled,"*
> *but you do not give them the things that*
> *are needed for the body, what does it profit?*
> (2:15-16)

James writes this to people who are poor and oppressed. Members of the church were being dragged into court by the rich and being taken advantage of by wealthy landowners. So the reality of their economic struggles makes for an accurate depiction of his question. It hits close to home when the people are truly in need of food and clothing in their daily lives. And to make it just a bit more personal, James says that it's a brother or sister who's naked and destitute. As genuine as this situation is that James poses, we can relate as we see the same destitution thousands of years later. We see it in the streets of our neighborhoods.

What do you think when you see people like this on this street? Are you moved with compassion? Do you see their need? Or do you simply look away? James depicts one who responds to the needy by saying, "Depart in peace, be warmed and filled." Has this person really done anything? He said something, but to what avail? It wasn't even prayer—

just a few pious words empty of any meaningful action. Just lip service.

Remember the words of Jesus:

These people draw near to Me with their mouth, and honor Me with their lips, but their heart is far from Me. (Matthew 15:8)

It's all about the condition of the heart. If we have a heart for God, there will be action. If our hearts aren't in it, we serve only with our words; it's a passive faith, a faith that gets nothing done, a faith that's good for nothing, as James says:

Thus also faith by itself, if it does not have works is dead. (James 2:17)

It's the goodness of God in us that brings about action. Works is the authenticator of faith.

There's a story about an old boatman who painted "Faith" on one oar of his rowboat and "Works" on the other. He was asked his reason for this. To answer, he slipped the Faith oar into the water and rowed. The boat, of course, moved only in a tight circle. Returning to the dock, the boatman said, "Now let's try Works without Faith, and see what happens." The boatman rowed with only the Works oar in the water. Again, the boat made a tight circle, this time in the opposite direction. What he was illustrating is clear: To move forward—whether in the man's boat crossing the lake, or in the Christian life—one needs both Faith and Works operating simultaneously.

Faith is the primary stance of the Christian life, and works are a way of life:

> *But someone will say, "You have faith and I have works." Show me your faith without your works, and I will show you my faith by my works.* (2:18)

Here James is saying to the person claiming faith to go ahead and show their faith without works (as if that were possible), and that he, in turn, would show his faith by his works. We won't live it if we don't believe it. Simple math, right? *Faith equals works.* Or better yet, cause and effect. This is his basis, on the theological unity of the two.

If we tossed a pebble into a pond, what would happen? The impact would send ripples across the surface of the water, right? So imagine what happens when genuine faith impacts the heart of a believer. The ripples of God's goodness will spread to everyone the believer encounters.

Let's look further:

You believe there is one God, you do well.
Even the demons believe and tremble.
(2:19)

Here James continues to condemn unfruitful faith by comparing the professing Christian to the entities of darkness. Even the demons believe in the existence of God, but nothing comes from their belief. James equates a faith without works to the faith of a demon! Oh, these demons tremble, because their fear is real, and their faith is substantiated. But it's not a saving faith.

James then concludes with his estimation that faith without works is dead—that an unfruitful faith is not a genuine faith.

Or perhaps there's *some* faith there, a minimal faith that produces little, because of the lack of cultivation and trust. This is the Christian who continues to struggle (winning and losing) between carnal desires and spiritual obedience. I illustrated this earlier with the fisherman who trained his two dogs to fight on command. Which dog won? The one he fed. We must deny the flesh daily and surrender our minds to the Spirit. When our minds are preoccupied with the flesh, we're in effect sitting on our spiritual hands. That's right where Satan likes us to be. He loves half-hearted Christians who produce the minimum of their potential in the Lord. Satan knows we're out of his reach, but he's happy to see that we're doing nothing to deter others from his grasp.

We must always look to feed our faith by drawing on God. We must meditate on His law day and night so His goodness will be manifested in us for the lost to see. Satan loves unfruitful Christians— Christians who don't make waves. Speaking of waves, let's revisit cause and effect. The impact of the pebble on the water's surface will cause a rippling effect. Now imagine the goodness of God landing in the heart of a believer who has little faith. Ripples, right? Now imagine the goodness of God landing in the heart of a believer who has great faith. Waves, right? Waves of God's goodness! That's who we want to be for God. We want to make waves in this world for Jesus.

James doesn't object to faith; he objects only to faith that's not accompanied by action. He wants Christians to have faith that works. Faith without deeds is mere lip service.

We're new creations in Christ, spiritually minded to walk in a faith that produces good works:

We are created in Christ Jesus to do good works, which God prepared in advance for us to do, that we should walk in them.
(Ephesians 2:10)

This is His purpose of goodness in us, because this is the way we should walk. Our deeds don't necessarily have to be over the top; sometimes it's just an encouraging word, a helping hand, a sensitive ear, a small act of hospitality—any opportunity to be of service or to share the gospel. The challenge for us is to be alert for these opportunities and not see them as interruptions or inconveniences, but as occasions for us to do the good works God has planned for us.

This is a faithful saying, and these things I want you to affirm constantly, that those who have believed on God should be careful to maintain good works. These things are good and profitable to men.
(Titus 3:8)

We're ambassadors for Christ. We're set apart as sons and daughters to do the will of God. So, we're stewards of God's goodness. Since He's the source of all that's good, let's be available and look forward to the work He has planned for us. God is good!

8

Faithfulness

F aithfulness is defined as being firm in adherence to promises or in observance to duty.

I love that this is a two-part definition. As for the first part, when I think of someone who's firm in adherence to promises made, only One comes to my mind:

> *Every word of God is true; He is a shield to those who put their trust in Him.*
> (Proverbs 30:5)

Now if every word of God is true and pure, then His Word can be counted on when He says, "I will give you a new heart and put a new spirit within you; I will take the heart of stone out of your flesh and give you a heart of flesh" (Ezekiel 36:26). We not only know this to be true by His Word, but because when we remember taking Christ to be our Savior and allowing His Spirit to work in our lives, we experienced it. We were witnesses to the power of God in us.

God also promises forgiveness:

If we confess our sins, He is faithful and just to forgive us our sins and to cleanse us from all unrighteousness. (1 John 1:9)

As far as the east is from the west—that's how far He promises to remove our sin from us (Psalm 103:12).

His promises go on and on, and He firmly adheres to them because He's unchanging. He's the same today as He was yesterday, and the same as He'll continue to be forevermore. When it comes to promises, only God can faithfully uphold them.

Now the second half of faithfulness defined is more fitting for us. If we hope to do well in being firm in adherence to duty, it's going to take the divine character of God's faithfulness at work in our lives. We're going to have to trust—and we *can* trust, because we've already established that God is trustworthy. So now we must look to the spiritual fruit of faithfulness found in God to exceed our limited faith, and break the barrier that keeps us from trusting beyond what we can see.

Seeing is believing—that's a popular saying, and its meaning is held by those without faith. By this philosophy, we're limited by our own natural ability and are denied the freedom that is just out of our sight. For the believer, this is not the order of things. Faith is the ability to trust what we cannot see. Faith is how we get over the walls of fear. If we're going to live by every word that proceeds from the mouth of God, we'll have to make leaps of faith and trust God for where our feet will fall.

For the Christian, we must walk by faith and not by sight. Otherwise we'll fail in observing our duty. To better understand faithfulness in our observance of duty, let's look to the parable of the talents, and walk with Brother Matthew as he witnesses to Jesus's teaching:

> *For the kingdom of heaven is like a man traveling to a far country, who called his own servants and delivered his goods to them. And to one he gave five talents, to another two, and to another one, to each according to his own ability; and immediately he went on a journey. Then he who had received the five talents went and traded with them, and made another*

five talents. And likewise, he who had received two, gained two more also. But he who had received one, went and dug in the ground, and hid his Lord's money. After a long time the Lord of those servants came and settled accounts with them.

So he who had received five talents came and brought five other talents, saying, "Lord, you delivered me five talents; look, I have gained five more talents besides them." His lord said to him, "Well done, good and faithful servant; you were faithful over a few things, I will make you a ruler over many things. Enter into the joy of your lord." He also who had received two talents came and said, "Lord, you delivered to me two talents; look, I have gained two more talents besides them." His lord said to him, "Well done, good and faithful servant; you have been faithful over a few things, I will make you a ruler over many things. Enter into the joy of your lord."

Then he who had received the one talent came and said, "Lord, I knew you to be a hard man, reaping where you have not sown and gathering where you have not scattered seed, and I was afraid and went and hid your talent in the ground. Look, there you have what is yours."

*But his lord answered and said to him,
"You wicked and lazy servant, you knew
that I reap where I have not sown, and
gather where I have not scattered seed. So
you ought to have deposited my money
with the bankers, and at my coming I
would have received back my own with
interest. Therefore take the talent from
him, and give it to him who has ten talents.*

*"For everyone who has, more will be given,
and he will have abundance; but from him
who does not have, even what he has will
be taken away. And cast the unprofitable
servant into the outer darkness. There will
be weeping and gnashing of teeth."*
(Matthew 25:14-30)

Let's look again at how Jesus begins this passage:

*For the kingdom heaven is like a man
traveling to a far country, who called his
own servants and delivered his goods to
them.* (25:14)

The man traveling to a far country refers to
Christ and His ascension to heaven. The servants
this man called represent the body of Christ. The
goods this man delivered to his servants represent
talents to improve. As Paul tells us about Christ,

"When He ascended on high, He led captivity captive and gave gifts to all men" (Ephesians 4:8). So Jesus leaves us with gifts—talents, skills, abilities, etc.—until He returns.

His parable continues:

And to one he gave five talents to another two, and to another one, to each according to his own ability; and immediately he went on a journey. (Matthew 25:15)

Each of the servants was entrusted with his master's wealth and was responsible for handling it properly. Their master was wise in his distribution; this is why we see five talents given to one, and two to another, and just one to the last servant.

If we look around at other believers today, we can clearly see how much they differ in their range of skills and abilities. The duties we're to faithfully observe are suitable to our individual situations and gifts we receive. It's unity and diversity in one body, the body of Christ. We're all members of the same body, but all can't be the eye or the ear, right? Some of us must be the hand or the foot, but every part of the body is significant, as Peter says: "As each one has received a gift, minister it to one another, as good stewards of the manifold grace of God" (1 Peter 4:10).

So, the good that any of us have is from God, and along with that good He provides the ability for us to improve on that good.

Jesus continues His story:

Then he who had received the five talents went and traded with them, and made another five talents. And likewise he who had received two gained two more also.
(25:16-17)

At this point in the parable, we begin to see how the Lord's servants are divided into two categories: faithful or unfaithful. We start with the first two servants, who faithfully labored and made themselves busy with their master's business until his return. Both worked in proportion to what their master had gifted them with, and both doubled the amount received. Although the amount of their gifts or talents varied, they were equally faithful.

Then there's the unfaithful servant:

But he who had received one went and dug in the ground, and hid his lord's money.
(25:18)

This servant represents the behavior of all unfaithful and unfruitful people who fail to utilize their gifts and blessings, and who thereby fail to do what the Lord requires of them. They complain that they've received fewer talents than others. And because they cannot do as much—or because God didn't supply them enough—they do nothing. They refuse to see that God can use them in any situation. Again, it's not the size of the gift; it's about being faithful in applying it.

> *After a long time the lord of those servants came and settled accounts with them.*
> (25:19)

This speaks of Christ's second coming. When He returns, all will go before the judgment seat of Christ and give account of what we've done in the body. As Paul says, "We must *all* appear before the judgment seat of Christ" (2 Corinthians 5:10). There's no way around it; our Master will return, so we aim to be always pleasing to Him.

The parable begins picturing this judgment in this way:

> *So he who had received five talents came and brought five other talents, saying,*
> *"Lord, you delivered to me five talents; look,*

*I have gained five other talents besides
them."*(25:20)

Here's the first servant to settle his accounts
with his master. A moment later, the second servant
approaches in the exact same way:

*He also who had received two talents came
and said, "Lord, you delivered to me two
talents; look, I have gained two more talents
besides them."*(25:22)

See how these two approach with confidence,
immediately stating what they were given and then
reporting what they'd gained. This testifies to what
John wrote in his first epistle:

*Love has been perfected among us in this;
that we may have boldness in the day of
judgment; because as He is, so are we in
this world.*(1 John 4:17)

When we're operating according to our design—
which is to be in line with our Master's will—we can
approach His throne boldly, knowing that we're
faithful in His business. There's no fear in love, and
all we're really doing is extending God's grace (love)
to others. We're bringing comfort to others with the
comfort we first received from our Lord. So on that

day of judgment, we don't have to be ashamed; we can boldly come to the throne as His faithful servant.

In His parable, Jesus shows such confidence being vindicated in the master's response to the first servant (and quickly repeated almost word-for-word to the second servant):

> *His lord said to him, "Well done, good and faithful servant; you were faithful over a few things, I will make you ruler over many things. Enter into the joy of your lord."*
> (25:21; see also verse 23)

Wow! Can you imagine hearing that from Jesus? These represent those who faithfully received Christ, then faithfully trusted Christ to transform their heart and renew their mind, and who then walk faithfully with Him until His return. Well done indeed!

It begins and ends with trust. If we trust that God is who He says He is, and believe that all His promises are true, we can do this. Paul reminds us in his letter to the Philippians that He who has begun a good work in us will complete it until the day of Jesus Christ. We can be confident in this, since God is surely God and every word that comes from Him is true.

In contrast, look at the response of the unfaithful servant:

> *Then he who had received the one talent came and said, "Lord, I knew you to be a hard man, reaping where you have not sown, and gathering where you have not scattered seed. And I was afraid and went and hid your talent in the ground. Look, there you have what is yours."* (25:24-25)

This is the least gifted servant, and the only one of the three to not bear fruit. Remember that he represents *unfaithful* servants and not minimally talented servants, because his lack of service didn't stem from the size of his gift, but from his failure to use it. I've witnessed greatly gifted persons accomplish little for the kingdom, and I've seen those with limited gifting who do the seemingly impossible. It's all God! What He does in us is in direct proportion to what we surrender and take on in Him through faith. Having fewer talents is no excuse to do nothing; God can work with the least of us if we'll faithfully do our part.

That third servant's heart wasn't truly committed to his master. His attitude implied that his master was an oppressor, compelling his laborers to sow for him while he alone reaped the benefits.

This is the wrong attitude toward God, yet there are professing Christians who demonstrate this attitude. They see God as overbearing and hard, and some think He is unjust.

Don't ever think like that; it's the mindset of the unfaithful servant who thinks poorly and wrongly about God, as the story from Jesus quickly makes clear:

> *But his lord answered and said to him, "You wicked and lazy servant, you know that I reap where I have not sown, and gather where I have not scattered seed. So you ought to have deposited my money with the bankers, and at my coming I would have received back my own with interest."*(25:26-27)

"Wicked" and "lazy" are fitting terms for this servant. The first because he has such a bad opinion of his master, and the second because he refused to do anything productive with the talent he received. We're taught to give thanks in everything, and that doing so is the will of God. This is the attitude we should have. With it we can be clearly focus on what we have instead of what we don't have. When we don't appreciate the things of God's grace, we'll allow those things to be buried and become of no use.

The master in the story exposes the flimsiness of the servant's excuse by saying that if he were indeed as the servant reports him to be, then he would have acted differently with the money—depositing it with bankers for interest. But this servant's failure wasn't because the master was a hard man and the servant was afraid; it was simply that the servant was wicked and lazy.

So, the master says this:

"Therefore take the talent from him, and give it to him that has ten talents. For to everyone who has, more will be given and he will have abundance; but from him who does not have, even what he has will be taken away."(25:28-29)

This is the truth of what we can expect if we choose to be unfaithful with the gifts God gives us. If we're unworthy of His trust, He'll simply take back what was given to us and provide it for the trustworthy servant. We never want to bury God's blessings or contain them to ourselves like a reservoir does with water. On the contrary, we want to be a river, allowing His blessings to pour through us to others.

Martin Luther said, "God our Father has made all things depend on faith so that whoever has faith will have everything, and whoever does not will have nothing."

The master in the story concludes with this command:

"And cast the unprofitable servant into the outer darkness. There will be weeping and gnashing of teeth."(25:30)

Ouch!

Who is this unprofitable servant? He's the person who's of no service to our Jesus, our Lord and Master. If Jesus isn't your Master, then there'll be no place for you in His house. His kingdom is not yours. We touched on this a little with Brother James, when he asked if a faith without works can be a saving faith. We learned that the answer is no. This fact causes me to believe that the third servant in the parable, the one possessing the fewest gifts, was never really committed to his master. To accept Christ as Lord and Savior, we have to surrender our lives and wills to make room for a new Master.

So we want to heed the better examples of the faithful servants, taking the gifts and the skills and the abilities God gives us and applying them as the

Holy Spirit prompts us. It begins with having faith in our Creator, faith in our design, and then faithfully carrying out the purpose of our design.

Meanwhile, don't compare yourself with the next Christian. We're all in different places in our own walk with God. You may see that you're accomplishing more than another, and the sin of pride will quench your spirit and limit the growth within you. Or you may see that another has abundance on top of abundance of God's grace, and you become discouraged at the thought of trying to measure up.

Instead, look to Jesus! God will always supply us just what we need. God uses the ordinary to do the extraordinary. God used a little shepherd boy to slay a giant, and He made him a king.

Never give room for discouragement. Before we can be trusted in big things, we must be faithful in the little things. Neglected gifts perish; improved gifts multiply. So, let's be faithful in the moments afforded to us, and let's trust our future to God.

9

Gentleness
and Kindness

The character of God is perfect and complete in its wholeness. When we take on His character by the grace of the Holy Spirit, gentleness and kindness are added to us as a manifestation of God.

We don't get God in part; we get all of Him. Nevertheless, for one reason or another, gentleness and kindness are two characteristics of God that we don't commonly hear preached and taught. When I hear brothers and sisters testifying to God's power in them, it's always the fruit of love, joy, and peace; rarely do I hear them praise the power of His gentleness and kindness in them. This is not because those qualities aren't there; it's just that most of us don't choose to cultivate this area of the Spirit in our lives.

Why is that? Can it be we're viewing some characteristics of God as more significant than others? Is love or peace greater than gentleness and kindness?

If we were to view the nine characteristics listed as fruit of the Spirit as players on a championship sports team, would love and peace be as Kobi and Shaq were to the Lakers? Would joy and patience be equivalent to the Steve Young and Jerry Rice of the Niners? Are these the "standouts" or "stars" of the Spirit?

I think many of us have that perspective, but we shouldn't. All nine qualities in the fruit of the Spirit are "star" quality. All nine are equal in power and significance as they sum up God's character bearing fruit in our lives.

So we shouldn't desire one aspect of God over another. It's the wholeness of His character working in us that truly and completely sets us apart. Just as He seeks all of our heart, we're to seek all of Him. If we want to experience and witness the full magnitude of God's power in us, we must trust that each characteristic of God bearing fruit in us is as significant as any other.

Gentleness and kindness are among the fruit of the Spirit for good reason. History has produced rulers who didn't possess these qualities. Not just rulers, but everyday people as well. I say this because people are powerful, and people can be dangerous. That point is obvious regarding people in positions of power, but what about you and me? We possess the power through our words and deeds to help or harm others. It's our nature to hurt, tear down, and destroy. It's God's nature to help, strengthen, and build up.

Since He is mighty in power, He's wise to demonstrate and teach us that true strength applied gently can lift up what is tender. It takes a strong person to be gentle and kind. People tend to confuse gentleness and kindness with weakness, but this is a fallacy. After all, how does one apply gentleness to weakness? There's no power in weakness to be wary of—rather, it's the strong hand, not the weak one, that must learn to be gentle. This is important for Christians to understand, because we're a powerful people. We're heirs to the most powerful being in existence—God Almighty. We have access to supernatural strengths, and we must display them with supernatural gentleness and kindness:

Let your gentleness be evident to all men.
The Lord is at hand. (Philippians 4:5)

Why does Paul write this to the young church at Philippi? He wants them to understand that followers of Jesus Christ are distinguished by gentleness. Believers today also need to understand this. If we aren't kind and gentle, then we certainly won't be approachable. How will the lost recognize us as a beacon of hope? How will the body of Christ recognize family when they're standing in our midst? Imagine Jesus traveling city to city during His ministry here on earth; how do you see Him? What you see is what you want others to see when their gaze falls on you.

As ambassadors for Christ, our inherent duty is to deliver the good news during our time spent on earth. We won't be able to fulfill our duties as faithful servants of our Master's business if we quench the power of God's kindness and gentleness in us. We need to cultivate all the fruit of the Spirit in our daily lives so that when a person who's lost comes into our path, the gentle hand of God can reach out to that person and save their life. Only a gentle and kind person can speak the truth in a way that others can receive it.

Let's look to Brother John's word and walk, and learn from his witness of when Jesus had dealt kindly and gently with an adulterous woman and her accusers in a volatile situation:

Now early in the morning He came again into the temple, and all the people came to Him, and He sat down and taught them. Then the scribes and Pharisees brought to Him a woman caught in adultery. And when they had set her in His midst, they said to Him, "Teacher, this woman was caught in adultery, the very act. Now Moses, in the law, commanded us that such should be stoned. But what do You say?" This they said, testing Him, that they might have something of which to accuse Him. But Jesus stooped down and wrote on the ground with His finger, as though He did not hear.

So when they continued asking Him, He raised Himself up and said to them, "He who is without sin among you, let him throw a stone at her first." And again He stooped down and wrote on the ground. Then those who heard it, being convicted by their conscience, went out one by one, beginning with the oldest even to the last. And Jesus was left alone, and the woman

*standing in the midst. When Jesus had
raised Himself up and saw no one but the
woman, He said to her, "Woman, where are
those accusers of yours? Has no one
condemned you?"*

She said, "No one, Lord."

*And Jesus said to her, "Neither do I
condemn you; go and sin no more."*
(John 8:1-11)

Look again at the opening verses here:

*Now early in the morning He came again
into the temple, and all the people came to
Him, and He sat down and taught them.*
(8:1-2)

I enjoy the ordinariness of how this section of
Scripture begins. I don't picture Jesus with a
lunchbox in His hand, but I certainly see Him
heading off for a typical workday in the midst of His
ministry. It's early in the morning, and Jesus walks
over to the temple compound in Jerusalem just west
of the nearby Mount of Olives. In the temple, there's
a great court surrounded by porches and pillars. It's
a perimeter court designated for the Gentiles, since
they weren't permitted any closer access toward the
inner temple. I imagine Jesus sat down—the normal

posture for Jewish teachers—and He began to teach any and all who gathered. And then:

> *The scribes and Pharisees brought to Him a woman caught in adultery. And when they had set her in the midst, they said to Him, "Teacher, this woman was caught in adultery, the very act."*(8:3-4)

Jesus is in the middle of teaching when suddenly there's an interruption. And it's no minor interruption. The scribes (the copiers of the law) and the Pharisees (the strictest of the Jewish sects) come barging in on this scene with a captive woman in tow. The precise circumstances concerning this woman are vague, but it seems clear what kind of woman this is.

Adultery is a serious charge; however, if she were truly caught in the act of adultery, where was her accomplice? It takes two to commit adultery, right? Could it be that the man has fled and narrowly escaped justice? Or perhaps he was somehow involved with the scribes and Pharisees in using the woman in a plot to trap Jesus, and so the man was allowed to escape. Either way, it seems likely that the woman had a reputation as a prostitute, and the authorities had been overlooking her sinful practices—until now, when it might serve as an opportunity to entrap Jesus.

But for the record: Who really is this woman? She is you, and me, and everyone else who has ever been caught in their sin.

The Pharisees continue setting the trap as they tell Jesus,

> *"Now Moses, in the law, commanded us*
> *that such should be stoned. But what do*
> *You say?"*(8:5)

In this, however, the Pharisees were misapplying the law of Moses. To fulfill the law, they should have brought both the man and the woman forward for judgment. What they were attempting to do was illegal. For the law to be used so egregiously by experts shows that their concern wasn't really for justice; it was all about concocting erroneous charges against Jesus, as John indicates:

> *This they said, testing Him, that they might*
> *have something of which to accuse Him.*
> *But Jesus stooped down and wrote on the*
> *ground with His finger, as though He did*
> *not hear.* (8:6)

The hypocrites set a test for Jesus in the hope that He would misapply the law of Moses (which is actually what the hypocrites did with the law). They cannot find anything to discredit Jesus legally, so now they press Him with a plot to be able to accuse Him of being a lawbreaker. Scripture doesn't reveal what Jesus wrote on the ground with His finger, but since He is Lord, I believe He wrote something significant for the people surrounding Him to see.

> *So when they continued asking Him, He raised Himself up and said to them, "He who is without sin among you, let him throw a stone at her first."* (8:7)

Up to this point, the scribes and the Pharisees think they have Jesus right where they want Him. They've approached Him with a mob mentality, and they probably mistake His stooped posture as a sign of vulnerability. They continue their offensive questioning: "What do You say? What do You say?"—much like authorities do today when interrogating a suspect they're trying to crack.

In spite of their efforts, Jesus rises and wisely says, "He who is without sin among you, let him throw a stone at her first." Wow! I bet they weren't expecting to hear that. What a blow to their self-righteous egos! Jesus brought them back down to the reality of their condition. The truth is that even scribes and Pharisees—and all who claim to be holy—are not without sin.

And again He stooped down and wrote on the ground. (8:8)

What is Jesus writing? I wish I knew, but it's evident that it was meant only for those standing in His midst at that particular moment. Some think that He might have been listing the sins of the onlookers in the dirt. That's certainly within the power of our Lord, but we simply don't know what He wrote. What's clear, however, is that nothing else needed to be said. The power of His last statement exposed the truth, and the matter no longer needed to be pursued.

Then those who heard it, being convicted by their conscience, went out one by one, beginning with the oldest even to the last. And Jesus was left alone, and the woman standing in the midst. (8:9)

God's Word tells us that there are none good— not even one (Romans 3:10-12). That's a sobering truth. Any of us can place ourselves in that mob-crazed circle of stone-throwers and be faced with the same reality. We know this, yet we find ourselves at times primed to throw stones.

We mustn't approach other sinners with a higher mentality of judgment when there's only One on a higher plain who is fit to judge. And although Jesus would have been within the law to judge her according to her sin, He was kind and gentle:

> *When Jesus had raised Himself up and saw no one but the woman, He said to her, "Woman, where are those accusers of yours? Has no one condemned you?" She said, "No one, Lord." (8:10-11)*

Imagine the hearts of the accusers. I believe that the Pharisees' hearts were hardened. For the truth that Jesus on other occasions had delivered to them ("Hypocrite! First remove the plank from your own eye, and then you will see clearly to remove the speck from your brother's eye"—Matthew 7:5) was not well received. And now, not only were they foiled in their plans to falsely accuse Jesus as a lawbreaker, but they were exposed as not really wanting to turn from their sin. They grew angry because the Lord exposed their inner sin.

This is the case for many people today; they would prefer to live in darkness and snuff out the light than come to repentance.

Now consider the final words our Lord spoke to this woman:

And Jesus said to her, "Neither do I condemn you; go and sin no more."(8:11)

Praise the Lord! What great mercy!

"For God did not send His Son into the world to condemn the world, but that the world through Him might be saved."
(John 3:17)

We can testify to God's forgiveness in our own lives, so we can fully understand the pardon extended to this woman. Who are we to throw stones? We must resist the temptation to judge others and allow the Spirit of God's will in us to love them. Without the fruit of the Spirit—kindness and gentleness—we're left with the heartless hypocrisy of a Pharisee. We live in a harsh world, and now more than ever we need to extend the mercies and grace of God.

I was riding my bicycle this summer in my hometown of Santa Clarita. I'm blessed to live in an area where community planners have given ample consideration to bicycling. My city has an extensive bicycle route system that goes for miles and miles.

It's a blacktop road six to eight feet wide, with a yellow dotted line down the middle to separate bicycle traffic going each direction. It attracts a great number of riders, and on any given day I'll pass single riders, paired riders, and groups of as many as twenty.

So, I was riding down the bike path recently on a hot summer day when I noticed a large group of riders approaching from the opposite direction. However, rather than all moving to their side of the dotted yellow line to yield the other lane to me (which normally would happen), their formation was actually getting wider and occupying both lanes on the path. Then I realized that this was due to a large obstruction in the path—they were simply going around it, like a river's flow that parts around a large rock. I wondered why one or more of them couldn't just stop for a moment to remove this object, so other riders wouldn't get hurt.

As I got closer, I saw that the obstacle was a man passed out right in the middle of the bike path. He was sprawled across both lanes, leaving only about a foot of clearance for riders to pass by either his head or his feet. My heart was struck with compassion. I wasn't sure what to do, but I certainly couldn't just ignore him and keep going. It was *hot* out, and he was lying in direct sunlight on black asphalt.

I got off my bike and knelt near his feet. I took hold of his pant leg just above his shoe and started gently shaking him. "You all right? You all right?"

When he came around, I asked if he wanted me to call for help. He didn't. I suggested that he should at least get out of the sun. That got him to pop open one eye and look about confused. Once his bearings lined up, he was able to crawl off the asphalt into the shade of some hedges bordering the path, and there he lay.

I didn't know what God intended to do in this situation when I was getting off of my bike, but now that the moment has passed, I see that He simply wanted this man out of immediate danger—out of bicycle traffic and out of the hot sun. I know, because that's what happened. Just like I know that the man would still be lying in harm's way had I not surrendered the moment and allowed the Holy Spirit to work in my life. *Faith equals works.* Without faith, I ride by him like everyone else.

Remember, the challenge for us is to be alert for opportunities, seeing them not as interruptions or inconveniences but as occasions to do the good works God has planned for us. Also, as we discussed earlier, we need to cultivate *all* the fruit of the Spirit in our daily lives so that when a person who's lost comes into our path, the gentle hand of God can reach out to that person and save their life.

So, we see that for our Christian growth, it's essential to have all the characteristics of God bearing fruit in us. We may esteem one as greater than the other because of natural tendencies—we may exhibit joy more naturally than gentleness, for example—but everything in our natural ability is lacking. As we grow in a living relationship with Christ, we join His "super" to our "natural," and we begin to exceed the boundaries of our flesh. If we think we can have one but not the other, then we really don't have anything. God is God! And if we've been purchased by the blood of Christ and we surrender to His management—then God is God *in us*!

10

Love

Love overcomes the human condition of the heart. How can we exhibit God's character without love? We can't. It's impossible. How can joy, peace, patience, gentleness, goodness, kindness, faithfulness, and self-control be real and effective without love? All are empty without love's compelling power.

Though I speak with the tongues of men and of angels, but have not love, I have become sounding brass or a clanging cymbal. And though I have the gift of prophecy, and understand all mysteries and all knowledge, and though I have all faith, so that I could remove mountains, but not have love, I am nothing. And though I

bestow all my goods to feed the poor, and though I give my body to be burned, but have not love, I am nothing. Love suffers long and is kind; love does not envy; love does not parade itself, is not puffed up; does not behave rudely, does not seek its own, is not provoked, thinks no evil; does not rejoice in iniquity, but rejoices in truth; bears all things, believes all things, hopes all things, endures all things.
(1 Corinthians 13:1-7)

We can speak eloquently and with the sweet song of an angel, but if there's no love behind our words, we're just making noise. Love is the reason for the truth, it's the power behind our hope and faith, and it's the source of all things good. God is love. By and through love, we overcome. Without it we're nothing.

God loves us so much that He didn't hold back His Son:

For God so loved the world that He gave His only begotten Son, that whoever believes in Him should not perish but have everlasting life. (John 3:16)

God sent Him to endure death on the cross as our substitute, so that we can be with Him forever. This is the love God has for us, so that we can overcome sin, death, and the world and its ways, and so that we can reign with Him. What an amazing love we receive!

And so, as God's children, are we to bottle up His love and contain it in a reservoir to ourselves? Or do we extend His love and grace to our neighbor? As faithful sons and daughters, we serve our Father in His business of salvation as the faithful servants did for their master with the talents (in Matthew 25). We freely extend to our neighbor the grace God has given us. Only by the love of God working in us will His love be received by others.

In this faithful endeavor to reach others with God's love, we have to be Spirit-minded, renewed in our minds to overcome the strongholds of our flesh. By the love God has put in our hearts, we must see others in the same way that God sees them.

We are all God's children. To better understand this, let's walk with Brother Luke and learn from his witness of Jesus in the parable of the Good Samaritan.

And behold, a certain lawyer stood up and tested Him, saying, "Teacher, what shall I do to inherit eternal life?"

He said to him, "What is written in the law? What is your reading of it?"

So he answered and said, "You shall love the Lord your God with all your heart, with all your soul, with all your strength, and with all your mind, and your neighbor as yourself."

And He said to him, "You have answered rightly; do this and you will live."

But he, wanting to justify himself, said to Jesus, "And who is my neighbor?"

Then Jesus answered and said: "A certain man went down from Jerusalem to Jericho, and fell among thieves, who stripped him of his clothing, wounded him, and departed, leaving him half dead. Now by chance a certain priest came down that road. And when he saw him, he passed by on the other side. Likewise a Levite, when he arrived at the place, came and looked, and passed by on the other side. But a certain Samaritan, as he journeyed, came where he was. And when he saw him, he had compassion. So he went to him and bandaged his wounds, pouring on oil and wine; and he set him on his own animal, brought him to an inn, and took care of him. On the next day, when he departed, he took out two denarii, gave them to the innkeeper, and said to him, 'Take care of him; and whatever more you spend, when I come again, I will repay you.' So which of these three do you think was neighbor to him who fell among the thieves?"

And he said, "He who showed mercy on him."

Then Jesus said to him, "Go and do likewise." (Luke 10:25-37)

Let's look again at the opening verses here:

And behold, a certain lawyer stood up and tested Him saying, "Teacher, what must I do to inherit eternal life?"

He said to him, "What is written in the law? What is your reading of it?"

So he answered and said, "You shall love the Lord your God with all your heart, with all your soul, with all your strength, and with all your mind, and your neighbor as yourself."(10:25-27)

A certain lawyer—this is one who would be an expert in Jewish law. This lawyer's belief system is rooted in the Old Testament law; it's all he has ever known, along with the traditions passed down from his predecessors. Everything he has studied begins and ends with the law—even his conviction that eternal salvation is granted only to those who can uphold the law.

Had this lawyer concluded on his own that it's impossible to heed the letter of the law and thereby gain salvation? Or was he wanting to set Jesus up to teach something outside the law, thus opening Himself up to condemnation as a lawbreaker? I don't know. Either way, the man tests Jesus with a valid question: "What shall I do to inherit eternal life?"

Jesus, knowing this lawyer's heart, refers him to the law—the source that ultimately leads all of us to our need for grace. At some point we must all realize that God's perfect law can't be measured up to in our imperfect natures. We must seek out God's perfect grace to do what we cannot do for ourselves.

There was once a missionary preaching in China, and as he was teaching, a young man approached him and said, "What is that in your hand?"

"It's a measure," the missionary said, "and it's like your measure—it has ten divisions." (The Chinese traditionally divide their "foot" into ten "inches," not twelve.)

"What do you measure?" said the man.

"I measure longs and shorts—long hearts and short hearts. Sit down and I'll measure you." The man sat down, and the missionary began to measure. He took the first commandment: *Thou shalt have none other gods but Me.* "Is your heart shorter than this commandment or longer?"

The Chinese man said, "Oh, I'm afraid it's very much shorter."

As the missionary went through all the Ten Commandments in this way, the poor man found that his heart was altogether too short; he didn't measure up to any of them. "You see," the missionary said, "your heart is too short. How shall we make up the deficiency? Who'll supply what's wanting?" He then spoke to him about Jesus Christ—how He would make up the man's shortcomings, and how by our partaking of Christ's obedience it's just as if we'd kept the whole law ourselves.

So perhaps some child will say, "I cannot do God's commandments." Don't say "cannot" when we know that all things are possible through Christ.

There was a poor man whose hand was withered and powerless, and Christ said to him, "Stretch out your hand." Could the man do this? Not before Christ gave this command; but once the Son of God told him to stretch out his hand, He also gave him power to do so. God's biddings are God's enablings.

Suppose you had a piece of cold iron, and I said, "Make me a pretty thing out of that." You would say, "I can't bend that cold iron, but by melting it, something might be done." Our hearts have been likened to cold iron, and we need the love of God to melt it, to soften it. Only then can we keep God's commandments.

Jesus asked this lawyer to summarize his interpretation of the law. The lawyer answered well: "You shall love the Lord your God with all of your heart, with all of your soul, with all of your strength, and with all your mind." This is to say—love God above all else. Love Him more than mother and father, husband or wife, son and daughter, personal status, money, occupation, sex, sports, drugs, alcohol, fame, etc. Anything we put before Him is idolatry. Nothing goes before God; we're to love Him with everything. Why? Because He is worthy!

Then the lawyer concludes with this phrase: "and your neighbor as yourself." These two laws sum up the entirety of our success according to the Old Testament. If we can succeed in loving God with everything, and in loving our neighbor as ourselves, we're guaranteed God's glory in that which remains.

Jesus answered the lawyer, "You have answered rightly: do this and you will live." (10:28). Then the lawyer pressed Him further:

*But he, wanting to justify himself, said to
Jesus, "And who is my neighbor?"*(10:29)

To love God—Creator and Father of the life we
have now and the life we have to come, and our
source of hope, and our greatest benefactor—is one
thing. But to love our neighbor as ourselves? We
already have a difficult time surrendering our love
of self to the Lord's preeminence in our lives, and
now we also must love our neighbors as ourselves?
Are we measuring up to this? Perhaps with our
family or closest friends, and maybe even with
coworkers who we like. Sure, we love our neighbor,
as long as we get to decide who that neighbor is.

I'm sure the lawyer expected Jesus to answer that
fellow Jews were his neighbors, just as we also
consider our real "neighbors" to be those who
believe like we do. But we, like the lawyer, must gain
a better understanding of who our neighbor is.

*The Jesus answered and said, "A certain
man went down from Jerusalem to Jericho,
and fell among thieves, who stripped him
of his clothing, wounded him, and
departed, leaving him half dead."*(10:30)

The Lord presents a probable case based on the
reality of the circumstances occurring in that time.

The wisdom of this approach is that the Lord made the lawyer his own judge in this matter, and so bound him to come to terms with a judgment he might have previously disagreed with.

The road Jesus is talking about spans the fifteen miles separating Jerusalem from Jericho. It's a well-traveled route that isn't without its dangers. History denotes that criminals known as highwaymen would attack travelers on this road, take their property, and sometimes leave them for dead—exactly as in this situation Jesus describes.

> *"Now by chance a certain priest came down that road. And when he saw him, he passed by on the other side. Likewise a Levite, when he arrived at that place, came and looked, and passed by on the other side. But a certain Samaritan, as he journeyed, came where he was. And when he saw him, he had compassion."*(10:31-32)

Both the priest and the Levite came upon the injured man, but they chose to avoid him and his worsening circumstances. Perhaps they were running late for work. Or maybe the idea of helping a stranger under those conditions was simply unfathomable because it would take them out of their comfort zone. For one reason or another, both men moved on unfazed, leaving the injured man at the mercy of the next passerby.

Are we like this when we come across people in need throughout our daily travels? We see them on the roads we frequent. Are we too busy to stop? In too much of a hurry? Are we afraid to break out of our comfort zones to meet a person's needs? Do we just skirt the situation, as the priest and the Levite did, and tell ourselves, "Someone else will see to his needs"?

These two men were in the business of God. They were "holy" men. Priests were those who carried out temple services, and Levites were those who assisted the priests in these religious matters. Perhaps it was this condition of their holiness that bound these two from helping, since it went against their personal traditions. This is good for us to understand as we grow in our spiritual walk; we don't benefit from the traditions of men and the practice of rituals. We can quote Scripture all we want, but if we don't have a relationship with our Father, His words are powerless in us.

What a striking contrast we see in the actions of this Samaritan:

"But a certain Samaritan, as he journeyed, came where he was. And when he saw him,

he had compassion. So he went to him and bandaged his wounds, pouring on oil and wine; and he set him on his own animal, brought him to an inn, and took care of him. On the next day, when he departed, he took out two denarii, gave them to the innkeeper, and said to him, 'Take care of him; and whatever more you spend, when I come again, I will repay you.'" (10:33-35)

We see that the Samaritan is involved in a healthy relationship of faith with God. Remember, it's faith that leads to works. Love leads us to our faith. It's the love of God that compelled this Samaritan to not only treat and bandage the victim's wounds and safely deliver him to an inn, but also to go above and beyond what many of us would consider as sufficient; the Samaritan spent the night with the wounded man, then arranged for his further care in his absence. This is the power of God's love in the heart of the believer. This is the character of God in His children.

Jesus then questions the lawyer:

"So which of these three do you think was neighbor to him who fell among the thieves?" And he said, "He who showed mercy on him." Then Jesus said to him, "Go and do likewise." (10:36-37)

The lawyer, being a Jew, would have expected his Jewish counterparts, the priest and Levite, to be the heroes in this story. However, the injured man received mercy from someone the lawyer would have considered the least likely to help, since in those days the Jews despised Samaritans.

By now the lawyer understands (if he didn't already) that he can't inherit eternal life by keeping the law. He simply doesn't possess the grace in his natural character to love his neighbor as himself. We all need God's grace in salvation, and we all need His Spirit of love to uphold what He commands us.

This world is constructed with barriers of fear, selfishness, greed, hate, racism, and a broad spectrum of differences. In this environment we must hold onto God's promises and remember that He who is in us is greater than he who is in the world.

By God's love, we've overcome sin and death. By God's love we overcome ourselves and everything that exalts itself against the knowledge of God. Only by God's love can we see people as He sees people— as His children and our neighbor. We're compelled by His love.

When I married, I let go of "single man" pursuits. It wasn't a snap-of-the-fingers transition, even though I fully understood that my life was no longer a "me" thing but a "we" thing. It was a complete paradigm shift to consider another and then to incorporate that person into all my dealings. On so many levels, there were old ways sacrificed and new ways adopted. At first these changes seemed a bit overwhelming, but I faithfully put my best foot forward instead of trying to resist. Change is difficult for many of us, even when it's a good thing. Nevertheless, we want to cling to our old way of life because we know it, we're used to it, and the unknown element of who we're going to be in our new identity can be unsettling.

I'm happy to report that my faith has been rewarded. I've successfully put the "single man" away and have become "husband"—not just as a title, but as a way of life. This transformation didn't come about by my understanding of biblical principles on the marriage union. It's the love of God at the center of our marriage that compels me to be a good husband for my wife. It's love that brought the biblical truth of the marriage union off of the page and into my life. My marriage is the wonderful consequence of a loving relationship.

This is how we must approach Christianity. God's will and purpose for us will not be achieved by the institution of religion, but by the relationship we have in Jesus Christ. We're transformed by His love. It's the fruit of this relationship that moves His promises for an abundant life out of the Bible and into our lives.

> *For the love of Christ compels us.*
> (2 Corinthians 5:14)

Our works stem from our inner transformation. And our inner transformation stems from our relationship with Jesus.

11

Transformational Habits

L et's begin by getting our priorities straight. The first thing we need to understand is that Jesus is everything. We have to believe with all our hearts that everything is nothing without Jesus. He must come before everything. It's by this understanding that our paradigm will change. We must not resist and cling to our old ways. We have to step out in faith and allow God to restore us, and then take us where we can never go on our own.

Prayer

We should begin every day with prayer. If we're going to walk with Jesus, we have to talk with Jesus.

Let's run everything by Him—our thoughts, hopes, dreams, fears, and daily plans. We must let Him in on all our relationships and everything in our schedule. He's a good counselor, so let's ask Him to help us stand firm in the land of temptation, and to give us the courage to faithfully walk toward the narrow gate.

Let's be mindful of our blessings throughout the day, always looking for opportunities to give Him thanks. If we're simply driving down the road in our car, let's give Him thanks. Let's thank Him that we can drive and for the car we're driving. If we're walking, let's thank Him for being able to walk. If we're on crutches or in a wheelchair, let's give Him thanks. No matter our situation, He is still God—and thank God for that.

We're commanded to give God thanks in everything. It's a tough thing to do when things aren't going well, but the aim of His perfect will is still true, whether or not it's difficult and whether or not we understand it. Let's give Him thanks in spite of our adverse feelings. Being grateful helps us to be submissive to God. A heart of gratitude overcomes pride and enables us to see God's sovereignty. In this, we'll walk closer with Jesus and develop an inner sense of contentment, and with contentment comes joy. You'll notice that grumpy people never give thanks for anything.

When we meet various trials throughout the day, let's stop and pray. We should seek God's counsel in everything. Let's talk it up and build our relationship with Jesus. This is the most important relationship we'll ever have. When this relationship is healthy, all our other relationships will prosper.

Let's pray at the close of our day. Let's give thanks for the day and reflect upon it. This is a good time to implement a spiritual diagnostic examination. As we reflect, we can examine our conduct to see if and where God is bearing fruit in our lives. Where His character is evident, we can give thanks, and where it's not, we can give thanks for making us aware of a personal area that we can begin to surrender. This is key in recognizing and shaping our growth. It's a very conscious exercise at first, but as we're being transformed, it becomes a natural good habit.

His Word

In times past, God used messengers to reveal His holy nature to men. These messengers were called prophets, and God would speak through these prophets to establish His laws and call those who've strayed back into the obedience of His laws. He'd use the prophets to instruct the people about His holiness regarding His judgment of sin. Through the prophets He encouraged people to seek Him wholeheartedly in word and in deed, and He revealed the future of His will for them in the coming of the Messiah.

After being sent by God to the city of Nineveh, the prophet Jonah cried out there against the people, saying, "Yet forty days and Nineveh shall be overthrown!" How do you think the people of Nineveh responded? They believed God. Their hearts were convicted with the truth that their sins were leading to death, so they repented, returned to God, and lived. God spoke to the people through the prophet.

In a later time, in fulfillment of prophecy, the Messiah came, and God spoke directly to the people through His Son. God left His throne on high and appeared to us through the miracle of the virgin birth, and He then dwelt among us in the form of man. As God in man form, Jesus was the perfect example of obedience. He taught the people in word and deed how to live the abundant life that can be found only in the Father's will.

And being found in appearance as a man,
He humbled Himself and became obedient

to the point of death, even the death of the cross. (Philippians 2:8)

In pursuit of the Father's will, Jesus faithfully endured the cross so that we can be saved from eternal damnation and be reconciled to the Father as adopted heirs of the kingdom. Praise Jesus! Jesus was then resurrected to show the truth of His promise that He is indeed God—conqueror of sin and death—and He returned to His throne at the right hand of the Father. However, He doesn't leave His people defenseless, as He explained to His disciples:

Nevertheless I tell you the truth. It is to your advantage that I go away; for if I do not go away, the Helper will not come to you; but if I depart, I will send Him to you. (John 16:7)

God comes to us again in the form of the Holy Spirit. God now abides in us through His Spirit and teaches us. He has also—through divine commission—recorded His Word by faithful men. At one time God spoke to men through His prophets. He spoke to men at a later time through the prophetic revelation of the coming Messiah. And now, He speaks to us through the Holy Spirit and the Bible:

> *All Scripture is given by inspiration of God, and is profitable for doctrine, for reproof, for correction, for instruction in righteousness, that the man of God may be complete, thoroughly equipped for every good work.* (2 Timothy 3:16-17)

Let's read our Bible every day—and not only read, but study it. We study and learn, not for information, but transformation. We must set apart time daily to spend time in His Word. If we're morning people, let's carve time out of the morning to seek God in His Word. If we're evening people, let's prioritize our schedules to accommodate a relationship with God through His Word at night. God will speak to us in His Word. He will reveal His promises and truths and give us good understanding of our purpose as His children. There's a biblical solution to every single question and problem one can encounter in this world.

When Satan tried to tempt Jesus when He was hungry, Jesus answered, "Man shall not live by bread alone, but by every word that proceeds from the mouth of God" (Matthew 4:4).

God's Word is as essential for the spiritual life as food is for sustaining physical life. We rely on God's Word for the abundant life and for everlasting life. His Word is alive and moves in the hearts of believers. It's a guide—a treasure map, if you will. Let's allow God to guide us through the Scriptures every day. It will build our relationship with God as we seek Him in His Word.

Fellowship

Fellowship is another area of our Christian walk that suffers in the busyness of life. This, too, is something we must pursue daily. I know you're thinking, "How?" Because I'm already suggesting that you pray and study your Bible daily, not to mention that we all have family, work, school, and our favorite pastimes such as video games, TV shows, etc. So how do we make time daily for prayer, Bible study, and fellowship?

We must make the time by prioritizing. Here's a great illustration I found of what this means—in a mayonnaise jar.

There's a story told about a philosophy instructor who stood before his class one day with some items in front of him. As the class watched, he wordlessly picked up a large empty mayonnaise jar and proceeded to fill it up to the top with rocks about two inches in diameter. He then asked the students if the jar was full. They agreed that it was.

The professor then picked up a box of small pebbles and poured them into the jar. He shook the jar lightly. The pebbles, of course, rolled down into the openings between the rocks. The students laughed. Again, he asked his students if the jar was full, and they agreed that yes, it was.

The professor then picked up a container of sand and poured this into the jar. Of course, the sand filled up everything else. "Now," said the professor, "I want you to recognize that this is your life. The rocks are the most important things—your family, your health, and anything so important that if it were lost, you would be nearly destroyed. The pebbles are other things in life that matter, but on a smaller scale—things like your job, your house, your car. And the sand is everything else—the small stuff."

If you put the sand or the pebbles into the jar first, there's no room for the rocks. The same goes for your life. If you spend all your energy on the small stuff—material things, and what not—you'll never have room for the truly important things. Pay attention to the things that are critical in your life. Set your priorities, knowing that the rest is just pebbles and sand.

As God's children, we know that our relationship with Christ is the first rock going into the mayonnaise jar. We must prioritize our time to accommodate prayer, Bible study, and fellowship into our daily schedules. This is our faithful investment into the life given us by the One who endured the cross. The blessings from this far exceed those available from any other way we could prioritize our lives. When we apply these good habits, we're available to be transformed through the power of the Holy Spirit. God can and will use us to His glory when we make ourselves usable for Him. It's a tragic mistake to think we can do more with our lives than God can.

To fellowship with our brothers and sisters in Christ is a beautiful thing—a blessing. So we're told,

> Let us consider one another in order to stir up love and good works, not forsaking the assembly of ourselves together, as is the manner of some, but exhorting one another, and so much more as you see the day approaching. (Hebrews 10:24-25)

There's a great blessing when the body of Christ comes together. We do this at church services and other church functions, and in various small groups and meetings. In these encounters we experience the same mind in Christ in the presence of our church family, and from it we become encouraged as we encourage others through the sharing of worship, prayer, and friendship that we pour into each other.

We don't forsake these opportunities to come together, as is the habit of some. I imagine that many in the early church forsook such opportunities for fear of persecution. I believe fear on some level might hold back people today. If that's the case, we need to surrender that fear and allow God's perfect love to cast it out. Others who profess Christ with their mouth forsake opportunities to assemble with the body of Christ because their hearts belong to the world. These do not know the Lord.

We must assemble together so much more as we see the day approaching. It has been recorded in the Bible that the kingdom of heaven is at hand. We knew it was close thousands of years ago; how much closer is it now? Every man's life will come to an end in the mortal body, and his spirit will come before the judgment seat of Christ. So, let's come together at each and every opportunity to encourage each other, for the kingdom of heaven is at hand!

Two are better than one, because they have a good reward for their labor. For if they

fall, one will lift up his companion. But woe
to him who is alone when he falls, for he
has no one to help him up.
(Ecclesiastics 4:9-12)

This truth speaks to a more intimate form of fellowship—an individual fellowship between good friends, or one that's shared between a husband and his wife. I strongly encourage such intimate fellowship. The marriage union is truly a blessing. In a way that only a spouse can, my wife's love and encouragement and help give me the confidence and tangible support to grow in Christ. Through the power of the Holy Spirit, she brings a blessing in comfort and edification that builds me into a godly man and husband.

We can experience a similar blessing of comfort and edification in our intimate friendships with our brothers and sisters. There are things and circumstances that occur in a man's life that my brother can relate to as only another man can. I'm sure this is the same among our sisters in the faith.

As iron sharpens iron, so a man sharpens
the countenance of his friend.
(Proverbs 27:17)

This is the blessing of mutual counsel or discipling. In the fellowship of friendship or marriage, we encourage and better each other as we bear one another's burdens and make up for each other's defects.

For example, I'm the driver in my family. Whenever we travel by car, I get consumed with route direction, flow of traffic, and a timely arrival. However, I'm not so good with controlling my speed, though I can count on my wife to check me if that speed gets excessive. And in my eight years of marriage, I haven't suffered a single speeding ticket.

This is another blessing that stems from our intimate relationships—we help each other though accountability.

Again, we must pursue fellowship daily. We must get to church and build relationships among the body of Christ. I know this is especially important for men, since we tend to isolate ourselves. "Woe to him who is alone when he falls, for he has no one to help him up." Let's show up for each other and learn to help and be helped.

12

Disciple and Witness

At this point, we're maturing into faithful disciples and witnesses for Christ. This is how we walk in a world system that's ruled by Satan. We're no longer slaves of fear and sin. We're liberated in Christ! By His grace we've been set apart.

However, we haven't been removed from this world. So, we walk with Jesus as He walked during His ministry on earth.

In this book we've learned how to maximize God's power in us by and through the Holy Spirit. We've also learned the good habits we must implement daily so that *nothing* of this world and of the flesh will hinder out transformation and stunt our growth.

*Blessed is the man who endures
temptation; for when he has been
approved, he will receive the crown of life
which the Lord has promised to those who
love Him.* (James 1:12)

If we love Him, we'll follow Him. We'll think as
He thinks as we willingly take on the mind of Christ.
Our love for Him will compel us to obedience, and
by our faithfulness we'll triumph over temptation
and sin. For this we receive a crown. The crown
represents rulership—that we've conquered sin in
our bodies and we live on as we were designed.
We're set apart—we're in the world but not a part of
it.

We are lights in a dark place:

*You are the light of the world. A city that is
set on a hill cannot be hidden. Nor do they
light a lamp and put it under a basket, but
on a lampstand, and it gives light to all who
are in the house. Let your light shine so
before men, that they may see your good
works and glorify your Father in heaven.*
(Matthew 5:14-16)

This speaks to our witness in Christ. This is the
ultimate goal of our design. First, we become
disciples, and then we make disciples of others. We

want to be Christians who walk out the entirety of our potential. God doesn't want us to confine His grace and blessings only to ourselves; He wants us to extend it to others. For one reason or another, some of us will put Jesus in a bag and dole Him out only as we see fit. But we aren't lights of the world to be flicked on and off. We're to shine continuously—at all times and in every place. We have to let Jesus out of the bag!

My wife was summoned for jury duty not long ago. During the jury selection process, the attorneys asked pointed questions to the potential jurors so they could fill the jury box with the kind of people the attorneys thought would be most helpful to their side. That was perfectly understandable. This case involved a person suffering from a mental illness who'd committed a crime, and this court proceeding was to determine whether he should be housed in prison or an asylum for the criminally insane.

The first question to my wife was, "Should people with mental illness be forced to take their medication?"

"Yes," she replied, "but only after their spiritual condition has been addressed first."

"What do you mean?"

"I believe that Jesus can heal."

"And...what do you mean by that?"

"I mean He has the power to heal people. He healed lepers and cast out demons."

This answer got the bailiff's attention. He slowly turned from his post and leaned out to get a better look at this juror who was testifying in the name of Jesus.

The attorney continued, "So you're biased? You don't believe in modern medicine?"

"No, I just believe that Jesus can do anything."

My wife was thanked, and she was excused from jury duty. Later, in the hallway outside the courtroom, my wife was approached by a couple of people who shared that they were encouraged by her faith.

For others in that courtroom, perhaps none had even considered God until then. I'm sure this is a common occurrence in situations both inside and outside courtrooms. I'm grateful for my wife's faithfulness to let Jesus out of the bag in such a place. She brought Jesus to the forefront of a matter, then trusted the consequences to Him.

We're to shine our light before others, that they would see our good works and glorify our Father in heaven.

The darkness will not receive the light—it cannot comprehend it. But for the lost, we shine a beacon of hope in a dark place. We shine a light on the path to life.

In God's will for me, His highest priority is that I be in a relationship with Him. The same is true for you and for the next person. We come together by design to seek and save what was lost.

> *What do you think? If a man has a hundred sheep, and one of them goes astray, does he not leave the ninety-nine and go to the mountains to seek the one that is straying?* (Matthew 18:12)

We must embrace God and each other, and never let go. The kingdom of heaven is at hand! Where we are now is a vapor—let's make good use of what little time remains.

Let's pray to Him.

Let's seek Him in His Word.

Let's fellowship in His presence.

Let's witness to others, for His glory.

Let's worship our God with everything we have.

Let's walk!

Made in the USA
Middletown, DE
04 June 2021

41021429R00086